FROM:

DATE:

SANCTUARY!
finding security in our insecure world

FOR MEN

The quoted ideas expressed in this book (but not Scripture verses) are not, in all cases, exact quotations, as some have been edited for clarity and brevity. In all cases, the author has attempted to maintain the speaker's original intent. In some cases, quoted material for this book was obtained from secondary sources, primarily print media. While every effort was made to ensure the accuracy of these sources, the accuracy cannot be guaranteed. For additions, deletions, corrections, or clarifications in future editions of this text, please write Freeman-Smith.

Scripture quotations are taken from:

The Holy Bible, King James Version (KJV)

The Holy Bible, New International Version (NIV) Copyright © 1973, 1978, 1984, by International Bible Society. Used by permission of Zondervan Publishing House. All rights reserved.

The Holy Bible, New King James Version (NKJV) Copyright © 1982 by Thomas Nelson, Inc. Used by permission.

Holy Bible, New Living Translation, (NLT) copyright © 1996. Used by permission of Tyndale House Publishers, Inc., Wheaton, Illinois 60189. All rights reserved.

The Message (MSG)- This edition issued by contractual arrangement with NavPress, a division of The Navigators, U.S.A. Originally published by NavPress in English as THE MESSAGE: The Bible in Contemporary Language copyright 2002-2003 by Eugene Peterson. All rights reserved.

New Century Version®. (NCV) Copyright © 1987, 1988, 1991 by Word Publishing, a division of Thomas Nelson, Inc. All rights reserved. Used by permission.

The New American Standard Bible®, (NASB) Copyright © 1960, 1962, 1963, 1968, 1971, 1972, 1973, 1975, 1977, 1995 by The Lockman Foundation. Used by permission.

The Holy Bible, The Living Bible (TLB), Copyright © 1971 owned by assignment by Illinois Regional Bank N.A. (as trustee). Used by permission of Tyndale House Publishers, Inc., Wheaton, Illinois 60189. All rights reserved.

The Holman Christian Standard Bible™ (HCSB) Copyright © 1999, 2000, 2001 by Holman Bible Publishers. Used by permission.

Cover Design by Kim Russell / Wahoo Designs
Page Layout by Bart Dawson

ISBN 978-1-60587-347-3

Printed in the United States of America

SANCTUARY!
finding security in our insecure world

FOR MEN

INTRODUCTION

L ife would be so much easier (easier, but not better) if your faith were never challenged—if you never experienced doubts, or temptations, or worries, or frustrations. But it doesn't work that way. Hundreds of times each day, your faith is challenged as God provides you with opportunities to do the right thing by overcoming a negative emotion, or by extending a helping hand, or by speaking an encouraging word, or by doing a thousand other seemingly insignificant tasks that make your world a kinder, gentler, happier place. When these opportunities occur, you have a choice: you can either accept God's challenge and follow His path, or you can ignore His calling and live with the consequences. The ideas in this book will encourage you to do the right thing by following God's lead and by putting your faith to work.

To God, there are no insignificant acts of kindness. For Him, there are no small favors, no unimportant good deeds, no minor acts of mercy, and no inconsequential acts of obedience. To God, everything you do has major implications within His kingdom. He takes your actions seriously, and so should you.

This book contains devotional readings that are intended to remind you that God's provision is the ultimate security. The text is divided into 30 chapters, one for each day of the month. Each chapter contains Bible verses, quotations, brief essays, and timely tips, all of which can help you focus your thoughts on the countless blessings and opportunities that God has placed before you.

During the next 30 days, please try this experiment: read one chapter each morning. If you're a man who is already committed to a daily worship time, this book will enrich that experience. If you are not, the simple act of giving God a few minutes each morning will change the tone and direction of your life.

Your daily devotional time can be habit-forming, and it should be. The first few minutes of each day are invaluable. So treat them that way and offer them to God.

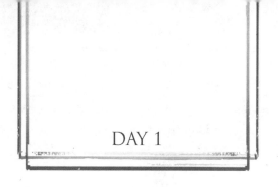

DAY 1

THE ULTIMATE SECURITY: GOD'S PROTECTION

Though I sit in darkness, the Lord will be my light.

—

MICAH 7:8 HCSB

Whatever hallway you're in—
no matter how long, how dark, or how scary—
God is right there with you.

—

BILL HYBELS

Have you ever faced challenges that seemed too big to handle? Have you ever faced big problems that, despite your best efforts, simply could not be solved? If so, you know how uncomfortable it is to feel helpless in the face of difficult circumstances. Thankfully, even when there's nowhere else to turn, you can turn your thoughts and prayers to God, and He will respond.

God's hand uplifts those who turn their hearts and prayers to Him. Count yourself among that number. When you do, you can live courageously and joyfully, knowing that "this too will pass"—but that God's love for you will not. And you can draw strength from the knowledge that you are a marvelous creation, loved, protected, and up-lifted by the ever-present hand of God.

OPEN YOUR HEART TO HIM

St. Augustine observed, "God loves each of us as if there were only one of us." Do you believe those words? Do you seek to have an intimate, one-on-one relationship with your Heavenly Father, or are you satisfied to keep Him at a "safe" distance?

Sometimes, in the crush of our daily duties, God may seem far away, but He is not. God is everywhere we have ever been and everywhere we will ever go. He is with us night and day; He knows our thoughts and our prayers. And, when we earnestly seek Him, we will find Him because He is here, waiting patiently for us to reach out to Him.

Today, as you carve out quiet moments of thanksgiving and praise for your Heavenly Father, open yourself to His presence and to His love. He is here, waiting. His love is here, always. Accept it—now—and be blessed.

MORE FROM GOD'S WORD ABOUT
HIS PROTECTION

Finally, my brethren, be strong in the Lord and in the power of His might. Put on the whole armor of God, that you may be able to stand against the wiles of the devil.

EPHESIANS 6:10-11 NKJV

The Lord your God in your midst, The Mighty One, will save; He will rejoice over you with gladness, He will quiet you with His love, He will rejoice over you with singing.

ZEPHANIAH 3:17 NKJV

God is my shield, saving those whose hearts are true and right.

PSALM 7:10 NLT

Those who trust the Lord are like Mount Zion, which sits unmoved forever. As the mountains surround Jerusalem, the Lord surrounds his people now and forever.

PSALM 125:1-2 NCV

But the Lord will be a refuge for His people.

JOEL 3:16 HCSB

MORE POWERFUL IDEAS ABOUT GOD'S PROTECTION

Adversity is always unexpected and unwelcomed. It is an intruder and a thief, and yet in the hands of God, adversity becomes the means through which His supernatural power is demonstrated.

CHARLES STANLEY

God helps those who help themselves, but there are times when we are quite incapable of helping ourselves. That's when God stoops down and gathers us in His arms like a mother lifts a sick child, and does for us what we cannot do for ourselves.

RUTH BELL GRAHAM

The only way to learn a strong faith is to endure great trials. I have learned my faith by standing firm amid the most severe of tests.

GEORGE MUELLER

A TIP FOR TODAY

Through good times and bad, God is always with you, and you are always protected.

A PRAYER FOR TODAY

Lord, sometimes life is difficult. Sometimes, I am worried, weary, or heartbroken. And sometimes, I encounter powerful temptations to disobey Your commandments. But, when I lift my eyes to You, Father, You strengthen me. When I am weak, You lift me up. Today, I will turn to You for strength, for hope, for direction, and for deliverance. Amen

TODAY'S THOUGHTS

My thoughts about God's love and His promise of protection.

_____

_____

_____

_____

_____

_____

_____

_____

DAY 2

WHERE TO TAKE
YOUR WORRIES

*Don't worry about anything, but in everything,
through prayer and petition with thanksgiving,
let your requests be made known to God.*

—

PHILIPPIANS 4:6 HCSB

God is bigger than your problems.
Whatever worries press upon you today,
put them in God's hands and leave them there.

—

BILLY GRAHAM

B ecause we have the ability to think, we also have the ability to worry. All of us, even the most faithful believers, are plagued by occasional periods of discouragement and doubt. Even though we hold tightly to God's promise of salvation—even though we sincerely believe in God's love and protection—we may find ourselves fretting over the countless details of everyday life.

Because of His humanity, Jesus understood the inevitability of worry. And He addressed the topic clearly and forcefully in the sixth chapter of Matthew:

> *Therefore I say to you, do not worry about your life, what you will eat or what you will drink; nor about your body, what you will put on. Is not life more than food and the body more than clothing? Look at the birds of the air, for they neither sow nor reap nor gather into barns; yet your heavenly Father feeds them. Are you not of more value than they? Which of you by worrying can add one cubit to his stature? . . . Therefore do not worry about tomorrow, for tomorrow will worry*

about its own things. Sufficient for the day is its own trouble. vv. 25-27, 34 NKJV

More often than not, our worries stem from an inability to focus and to trust. We fail to focus on a priceless gift from God: the profound, precious, present moment. Instead of thanking God for the blessings of this day, we choose to fret about two more ominous days: yesterday and tomorrow. We stew about the unfairness of the past, or we agonize about the uncertainty of the future. Such thinking stirs up negative feelings that prepare our hearts and minds for an equally destructive emotion: fear.

Our fears are rooted in a failure to trust. Instead of trusting God's plans for our lives, we fix our minds on countless troubles that might come to pass (but seldom do). A better strategy, of course, is to take God at His word by trusting His promises. Our Lord has promised that He will care for our needs—needs, by the way, that He understands far more completely than we do. God's Word is unambiguous; so, too, should be our trust in Him.

In Matthew 6, Jesus instructs us to live in day-tight compartments. He reminds us that each day has enough worries of its own without the added weight of yesterday's regrets or tomorrow's fears. Perhaps you feel disturbed by the past or threatened by the future. Perhaps you are concerned about your relationships, your health, or your finances. Or perhaps you are simply a "worrier" by nature.

If so, make Matthew 6 a regular part of your daily Bible reading. This beautiful passage will remind you that God still sits in His heaven and you are His beloved child. Then, perhaps, you will worry less and trust God more. And that's as it should be because God is trustworthy . . . and you are protected.

Today is mine. Tomorrow is none of my business.
If I peer anxiously into the fog of the future,
I will strain my spiritual eyes so that
I will not see clearly what is required of me now.

—

ELISABETH ELLIOTT

MORE FROM GOD'S WORD ABOUT
OVERCOMING ANXIETY

*I will be with you when you pass through the waters . . . when
you walk through the fire . . . the flame will not burn you. For
I the Lord your God, the Holy One of Israel, and your Savior.*

ISAIAH 43:2-3 HCSB

*Your heart must not be troubled. Believe in God; believe also
in Me.*

JOHN 14:1 HCSB

*Come to Me, all you who labor and are heavy laden, and I will
give you rest. Take My yoke upon you and learn from Me, for
I am gentle and lowly in heart, and you will find rest for your
souls. For My yoke is easy and My burden is light.*

MATTHEW 11:28-30 NKJV

*Be strong and courageous, and do the work. Don't be afraid or
discouraged, for the Lord God, my God, is with you. He won't
leave you or forsake you.*

1 CHRONICLES 28:20 HCSB

MORE POWERFUL IDEAS ABOUT WORRY

Today is the tomorrow we worried about yesterday.

DENNIS SWANBERG

Pray, and let God worry.

MARTIN LUTHER

Worry and anxiety are sand in the machinery of life; faith is the oil.

E. STANLEY JONES

Never yield to gloomy anticipation. Place your hope and confidence in God. He has no record of failure.

MRS. CHARLES E. COWMAN

A TIP FOR TODAY

You have worries, but God has solutions. Your challenge is to trust Him to solve the problems that you can't.

The beginning of anxiety is the end of faith, and the beginning of true faith is the end of anxiety.

GEORGE MUELLER

A PRAYER FOR TODAY

Lord, sometimes this world is a difficult place, and, as a frail human being, I am fearful. When I am worried, restore my faith. When I am anxious, turn my thoughts to You. When I grieve, touch my heart with Your enduring love. Give me the wisdom to trust in You, Father, and give me the courage to live a life of faith, not a life of fear. Amen

TODAY'S THOUGHTS

My thoughts about the need to trust God and to embrace the changes that He has placed along my path.

_____

_____

_____

_____

_____

_____

_____

_____

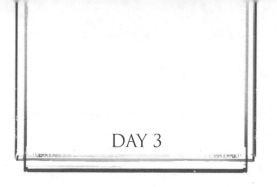

DAY 3

GOD'S PLAN AND
YOUR TOUGH TIMES

*"For I know the plans I have for you,"
declares the Lord, "plans to prosper you and not
to harm you, plans to give you hope and a future.
Then you will call upon me and come and pray to
me, and I will listen to you."*

—

JEREMIAH 29:11-12 NIV

God will not permit any troubles to come upon us
unless He has a specific plan by which great blessing
can come out of the difficulty.

—

PETER MARSHALL

It's an age-old riddle: Why does God allow us to endure tough times? After all, since we trust that God is all-powerful, and since we trust that His hand shapes our lives, why doesn't He simply rescue us—and our loved ones—from all hardship and pain?

God's Word teaches us again and again that He loves us and wants the best for us. And the Bible also teaches us that God is ever-present and always watchful. So why, we wonder, if God is really so concerned with every detail of our lives, does He permit us to endure emotions like grief, sadness, shame, or fear? And why does He allow tragic circumstances to invade the lives of good people? These questions perplex us, especially when times are tough.

On occasion, all of us face adversity, and throughout life, we all must endure life-changing personal losses that leave us breathless. When we pass through the dark valleys of life, we often ask, "Why me?" Sometimes, of course, the answer is obvious—sometimes we make mistakes, and we must pay for them. But on other occasions, when we have done nothing wrong, we wonder why God allows us to suffer.

Even when we cannot understand God's plans, we must trust them. And even when we are impatient for our situations to improve, we must trust God's timing. If we seek to live in accordance with His plan for our lives, we must continue to study His Word (in good times and bad), and we must be watchful for His signs, knowing that in time, He will lead us through the valleys, onward to the mountaintop.

So if you're a man who is enduring tough times, don't give up and don't give in. God still has glorious plans for you. So keep your eyes and ears open . . . as well as your heart.

FINDING NEW MEANING

Perhaps tough times have turned your world upside down. Maybe it seems to you as if everything in your life has been rearranged. Or perhaps your relationships and your responsibilities have been permanently altered. If so, you may come face to face with the daunting task of finding new purpose for your life. And God is willing to help.

God has an important plan for your life, and part of His plan may well be related to the tough times you're experiencing. After all, you've learned important, albeit hard-earned, lessons. And you're certainly wiser today than you were yesterday. So your suffering carries with it great potential: the potential for intense personal growth and the potential to help others.

As you begin to reorganize your life, look for ways to use your experiences for the betterment of others. When you do, you can rest assured that the course of your recovery will depend upon how quickly you discover new people to help and new reasons to live. And as you move through and beyond your own particular tough times, be mindful of this fact: as a survivor, you will have countless opportunities to serve others. By serving others, you will bring glory to God and meaning to the hardships you've endured.

MORE FROM GOD'S WORD ABOUT HIS PLAN

Who are those who fear the Lord? He will show them the path they should choose. They will live in prosperity, and their children will inherit the Promised Land.

PSALM 25:12-13 NLT

And we know that in all things God works for the good of those who love him, who have been called according to his purpose.

ROMANS 8:28 NIV

The steps of the Godly are directed by the Lord. He delights in every detail of their lives. Though they stumble, they will not fall, for the Lord holds them by the hand.

PSALM 37:23-24 NLT

It is God who works in you to will and to act according to his good purpose.

PHILIPPIANS 2:13 NIV

He replied, "Every plant that My heavenly Father didn't plant will be uprooted."

MATTHEW 15:13 HCSB

26

MORE POWERFUL IDEAS ABOUT GOD'S PLAN

Every misfortune, every failure, every loss may be transformed. God has the power to transform all misfortunes into "God-sends."

MRS. CHARLES E. COWMAN

Our heavenly Father never takes anything from his children unless he means to give them something better.

GEORGE MUELLER

Each problem is a God-appointed instructor.

CHARLES SWINDOLL

Our loving God uses difficulty in our lives to burn away the sin of self and build faith and spiritual power.

BILL BRIGHT

On the darkest day of your life, God is still in charge. Take comfort in that.

MARIE T. FREEMAN

A TIP FOR TODAY

Even when you can't understand God's plans, you must trust Him and never lose faith!

27

A PRAYER FOR TODAY

Dear Lord, even when I am discouraged, even when my heart is heavy, I will earnestly seek Your will for my life. You have a plan for me that I can never fully understand. But You understand. And I will trust You today, tomorrow, and forever. Amen

TODAY'S THOUGHTS

Answer this: Since I believe that God has a plan for my life, do I believe that He can help me overcome tough times and bring something good out of my hardships?

_____

_____

_____

_____

_____

_____

_____

_____

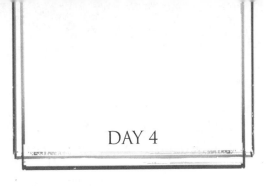

DAY 4

BEYOND FEAR

Indeed, God is my salvation.
I will trust [Him] and not be afraid.

—

ISAIAH 12:2 HCSB

He knows when we go into the storm,
He watches over us in the storm,
and He can bring us out of the storm
when His purposes have been fulfilled.

—

WARREN WIERSBE

All of us may find our courage tested by the inevitable disappointments and tragedies of life. After all, ours is a world filled with uncertainty, hardship, sickness, and danger. Old Man Trouble, it seems, is never too far from the front door.

When we focus upon our fears and our doubts, we may find many reasons to lie awake at night and fret about the uncertainties of the coming day. A better strategy, of course, is to focus not upon our fears, but instead upon our God.

God is as near as your next breath, and He is in control. He offers salvation to all His children, including you. God is your shield and your strength; you are His forever. So don't focus your thoughts upon the fears of the day. Instead, trust God's plan and His eternal love for you. And remember: God is good, and He has the last word.

GOD CAN HANDLE IT

It's a promise that is made over and over again in the Bible: whatever "it" is, God can handle it.

Life isn't always easy. Far from it! Sometimes, life can be very, very tough. But even then, even during our darkest moments, we're protected by a loving Heavenly Father. When we're worried, God can reassure us; when we're sad, God can comfort us. When our hearts are broken, God is not just near; He is here. So we must lift our thoughts and prayers to Him. When we do, He will answer our prayers. Why? Because He is our Shepherd, and He has promised to protect us now and forever.

Do not build up obstacles in your imagination.
Difficulties must be studied and dealt with,
but they must not be magnified by fear.

—

NORMAN VINCENT PEALE

MORE FROM GOD'S WORD ABOUT
OVERCOMING FEAR

Even when I go through the darkest valley, I fear [no] danger, for You are with me.

PSALM 23:4 HCSB

Don't be afraid. Only believe.

MARK 5:36 HCSB

For I, the Lord your God, hold your right hand and say to you: Do not fear, I will help you.

ISAIAH 41:13 HCSB

I sought the Lord, and He heard me, and delivered me from all my fears.

PSALM 34:4 NKJV

Do not fear, for I am with you; do not be afraid, for I am your God. I will strengthen you; I will help you; I will hold on to you with My righteous right hand.

ISAIAH 41:10 HCSB

MORE POWERFUL IDEAS ABOUT
OVERCOMING FEAR

Faith is stronger than fear.

JOHN MAXWELL

The Bible is a Christian's guidebook, and I believe the knowledge it sheds on pain and suffering is the great antidote to fear for suffering people. Knowledge can dissolve fear as light destroys darkness.

PHILIP YANCEY

People who focus on their fears don't grow. They become paralyzed.

JOHN MAXWELL

Are you fearful? First, bow your head and pray for God's strength. Then, raise your head and look Old Man Trouble squarely in the eye. Chances are, Old Man Trouble will blink.

JIM GALLERY

A TIP FOR TODAY

If you're feeling fearful or anxious, you must trust God to solve the problems that are simply too big for you to solve.

A PRAYER FOR TODAY

Dear Lord, when I am fearful, keep me mindful that You are my protector and my salvation. Thank You, Father, for a perfect love that casts out fear. Because of You, I can live courageously and faithfully this day and every day. Amen

TODAY'S THOUGHTS

My thoughts about the need to trust God in every situation.

_____

_____

_____

_____

_____

_____

_____

_____

_____

_____

DAY 5

OVERCOMING
TEMPTATION

*No temptation has overtaken you except what is
common to humanity. God is faithful and He will
not allow you to be tempted beyond what you are
able, but with the temptation He will also provide
a way of escape, so that you are able to bear it.*

—

1 CORINTHIANS 10:13 HCSB

Ask Christ to come into your heart to forgive you
and help you. When you do, Christ will take up
residence in your life by His Holy Spirit,
and when you face temptations and trials,
you will no longer face them alone.

—

BILLY GRAHAM

It's inevitable: today you will be tempted by somebody or something—in fact, you will probably be tempted on countless occasions. Why? Because you live in a world that's filled to the brim with temptations and addictions that are intended to lead you far, far away from God.

Here in the 21st century, temptations are now completely and thoroughly woven into the fabric of everyday life. Seductive images are everywhere; subtle messages tell you that it's okay to sin "just a little"; and to make matters even worse, society doesn't just seem to endorse godlessness, it actually seems to reward it. Society spews forth a wide range of messages, all of which imply that it's okay to rebel against God. These messages, of course, are extremely dangerous and completely untrue.

How can you stand up against society's tidal wave of temptations? By learning to direct your thoughts and your eyes in ways that are pleasing to God . . . and by relying upon Him to deliver you from the evils that threaten you.

And here's the good news: the Creator has promised (not implied, not suggested, not insinuated—He has promised!) that with His help, you can resist every single temptation that confronts you.

When it comes to fighting Satan, you are never alone. God is always with you, and if you do your part He will do His part. But what, precisely, is your part? A good starting point is simply learning how to recognize the subtle temptations that surround you. The images of immorality are ubiquitous, and they're intended to hijack your mind, your heart, your pocketbook, your life, and your soul. Don't let them do it.

Satan is both industrious and creative; he's working 24/7, and he's causing pain, heartache, trauma, and tragedy in more ways than ever before. You, as a Christian man of God, must remain watchful and strong—starting today, and ending never.

The higher the hill, the stronger the wind:
so the loftier the life,
the stronger the enemy's temptations.

—

JOHN WYCLIFFE

37

MORE FROM GOD'S WORD ABOUT TEMPTATION

Be sober! Be on the alert! Your adversary the Devil is prowling around like a roaring lion, looking for anyone he can devour.

1 PETER 5:8 HCSB

Put on the full armor of God so that you can stand against the tactics of the Devil.

EPHESIANS 6:11 HCSB

Stay awake and pray, so that you won't enter into temptation. The spirit is willing, but the flesh is weak.

MATTHEW 26:41 HCSB

The Spirit's law of life in Christ Jesus has set you free from the law of sin and of death.

ROMANS 8:2 HCSB

Do not be deceived: "Bad company corrupts good morals."

1 CORINTHIANS 15:33 HCSB

MORE POWERFUL IDEAS ABOUT TEMPTATION

The Bible teaches us in times of temptation there is one command: Flee! Get away from it, for every struggle against lust using only one's own strength is doomed to failure.

DIETRICH BONHOEFFER

Many jokes are made about the devil, but the devil is no joke. He is called a deceiver. In order to accomplish his purpose, the devil blinds people to their need for Christ. Two forces are at work in our world—the forces of Christ and the forces of the devil—and you are asked to choose.

BILLY GRAHAM

Every time we are tempted in life, it will be by something immediate. It will be something that will suggest to us that we need to postpone the more important for the more urgent.

FRANKLIN GRAHAM

A TIP FOR TODAY

Because you live in a temptation-filled world, you must guard your eyes, your thoughts, and your heart—all day, every day.

A PRAYER FOR TODAY

Dear Lord, this world is filled with temptations, distractions, and frustrations. When I turn my thoughts away from You and Your Word, Lord, I suffer bitter consequences. But, when I trust in Your commandments, I am safe. Direct my path far from the temptations and distractions of the world. Let me discover Your will and follow it, Dear Lord, this day and always. Amen

TODAY'S THOUGHTS

My thoughts about the dangers of the world's distractions and temptations.

_____

_____

_____

_____

_____

_____

_____

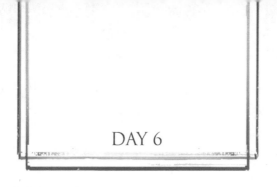

DAY 6

DISCOVERING PEACE

And the peace of God, which surpasses all understanding, will guard your hearts and minds through Christ Jesus. Finally, brethren, whatever things are true, whatever things are noble, whatever things are just, whatever things are pure, whatever things are lovely, whatever things are of good report, if there is any virtue and if there is anything praiseworthy—meditate on these things.

—

PHILIPPIANS 4:7-8 NKJV

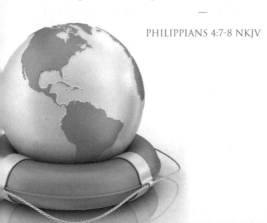

The better acquainted you become with God, the less
tensions you feel and the more peace you possess.

—

CHARLES ALLEN

Have you found the lasting peace that can—and
should—be yours through Jesus Christ? Or are
you still chasing the illusion of "peace and happi-
ness" that the world promises but cannot deliver?

The beautiful words of John 14:27 promise that Jesus offers peace, not as the world gives, but as He alone
gives: "Peace I leave with you. My peace I give to you. I do
not give to you as the world gives. Your heart must not be
troubled or fearful" (HCSB). Your challenge is to accept
Christ's peace into your heart and then, as best you can, to
share His peace with your neighbors. But sometimes, that's
easier said than done.

If you are a person with lots of obligations and plenty
of responsibilities, it is simply a fact of life: you worry. From
time to time, you worry about finances, safety, health,
home, family, or about countless other concerns, some
great and some small. Where is the best place to take your
worries? Take them to God . . . and leave them there.

The Scottish preacher George McDonald observed,
"It has been well said that no man ever sank under the
burden of the day. It is when tomorrow's burden is added

to the burden of today that the weight is more than a man can bear. Never load yourselves so, my friends. If you find yourselves so loaded, at least remember this: it is your own doing, not God's. He begs you to leave the future to Him."

Today, as a gift to yourself, to your family, and to your friends, claim the inner peace that is your spiritual birthright: the peace of Jesus Christ. Christ is standing at the door, waiting patiently for you to invite Him to reign over your heart. His eternal peace is offered freely. Claim it today.

TIME FOR SILENCE

The world seems to grow louder day by day, and our senses seem to be invaded at every turn. But, if we allow the distractions of a clamorous society to separate us from God's peace, we do ourselves a profound disservice. Our task, as dutiful believers, is to carve out moments of silence in a world filled with noise.

If we are to maintain righteous minds and compassionate hearts, we must take time each day for prayer and for meditation. We must make ourselves still in the presence of our Creator. We must quiet our minds and our hearts so that we might sense God's will and His love.

Has the busy pace of life robbed you of the peace that God has promised? If so, it's time to reorder your priorities and your life. Nothing is more important than the time you spend with your Heavenly Father. So be still and claim the inner peace that is found in the silent moments you spend with God. His peace is offered freely; it has been paid for in full; it is yours for the asking. So ask. And then share.

In the center of a hurricane there is
absolute quiet and peace.
There is no safer place than in the center
of the will of God.

—

CORRIE TEN BOOM

MORE FROM GOD'S WORD ABOUT PEACE

If possible, on your part, live at peace with everyone.

ROMANS 12:18 HCSB

Abundant peace belongs to those who love Your instruction; nothing makes them stumble.

PSALM 119:165 HCSB

Blessed are the peacemakers, for they shall be called sons of God.

MATTHEW 5:9 NKJV

And suddenly there was with the angel a multitude of the heavenly host praising God and saying: "Glory to God in the highest, and on earth peace, goodwill toward men!"

LUKE 2:13-14 NKJV

So then, we must pursue what promotes peace and what builds up one another.

ROMANS 14:19 HCSB

MORE POWERFUL IDEAS ABOUT
FINDING PEACE

A great many people are trying to make peace, but that has already been done. God has not left it for us to do; all we have to do is to enter into it.

D. L. MOODY

For Jesus peace seems to have meant not the absence of struggle but the presence of love.

FREDERICK BUECHNER

The Christian has a deep, silent, hidden peace, which the world sees not, like some well in a retired and shady place.

JOHN HENRY CARDINAL NEWMAN

A TIP FOR TODAY

God's peace surpasses human understanding. When you accept His peace, it will revolutionize your life.

That peace, which has been described and which believers enjoy, is a participation of the peace which their glorious Lord and Master himself enjoys.

JONATHAN EDWARDS

46

A PRAYER FOR TODAY

Dear Lord, when I turn my thoughts and prayers to You, I feel the peace that You intend for my life. But sometimes, Lord, I distance myself from You; sometimes, I am distracted by the busyness of the day or the demands of the moment. When I am worried or anxious, Father, turn my thoughts back to You. You are the Giver of all things good, and You give me peace when I draw close to You. Help me to trust Your will, to follow Your commands, and to accept Your peace, today and forever. Amen

TODAY'S THOUGHTS

My thoughts about what it means to experience "the peace which surpasses all understanding."

_____

_____

_____

_____

_____

_____

_____

DAY 7

TIME TO GET BUSY

*And whatever you do, do it heartily,
as to the Lord and not to men.*

—

COLOSSIANS 3:23 NKJV

Let us not be content to wait and see
what will happen, but give us the determination
to make the right things happen.

—

PETER MARSHALL

It isn't easy to overcome tough times—it takes hard work and lots of it. So if you're facing adversity of any kind, you can be sure that God has important work for you to do . . . but He won't make you do it. Since the days of Adam and Eve, God has allowed His children to make choices for themselves, and so it is with you. You can either dig in and work hard, or you can retreat to the couch, click on the TV, and hope things get better on their own.

The Bible instructs us that we can learn an important lesson from a surprising source: ants. Ants are among nature's most industrious creatures. They do their work without supervision, rumination, or hesitation. We should do likewise. When times are tough, we must summon the courage and determination to work ourselves out of trouble.

God has created a world in which diligence is rewarded and sloth is not. So whatever you choose to do, do it with commitment, excitement, and vigor. God didn't create you for a life of mediocrity or pain; He created you for far greater things. Reaching for greater things—and defeating tough times—usually requires work and lots of it, which is perfectly fine with God. After all, He knows that you're up to the task, and He still has big plans for you. Very big plans . . .

WHEREVER YOU ARE, WORK HARD

Wherever you find yourself, whatever your job description, do your work, and do it with all your heart. When you do, you will most certainly win the recognition of your peers. But more importantly, God will bless your efforts and use you in ways that only He can understand. So do your work with focus and dedication. And leave the rest up to God.

It is by acts and not by ideas that people live.

—

HARRY EMERSON FOSDICK

MORE FROM GOD'S WORD ABOUT
THE NEED TO TAKE ACTION

For the Kingdom of God is not just fancy talk; it is living by God's power.

1 CORINTHIANS 4:20 NLT

Therefore, get your minds ready for action, being self-disciplined, and set your hope completely on the grace to be brought to you at the revelation of Jesus Christ.

1 PETER 1:13 HCSB

But prove yourselves doers of the word, and not merely hearers.

JAMES 1:22 NASB

Are there those among you who are truly wise and understanding? Then they should show it by living right and doing good things with a gentleness that comes from wisdom.

JAMES 3:13 NCV

The prudent see danger and take refuge, but the simple keep going and suffer from it.

PROVERBS 27:12 NIV

51

MORE POWERFUL IDEAS ABOUT
THE NEED TO TAKE ACTION

Action springs not from thought, but from a readiness for responsibility.

DIETRICH BONHOEFFER

God has lots of folks who intend to go to work for Him "some day." What He needs is more people who are willing to work for Him this day.

MARIE T. FREEMAN

Paul did one thing. Most of us dabble in forty things. Are you a doer or a dabbler?

VANCE HAVNER

A TIP FOR TODAY

Today, pick out one important obligation that you've been putting off. Then, take at least one specific step toward the completion of that task.

Logic will not change an emotion, but action will.

ZIG ZIGLAR

Pray as if it's all up to God, and work as if it's all up to you.

ANONYMOUS

A PRAYER FOR TODAY

Heavenly Father, when I am fearful, keep me mindful that You are my protector and my salvation. Give me strength, Lord, to face the challenges of this day as I gain my courage from You. Amen

TODAY'S THOUGHTS

My thoughts about an important challenge that I've been avoiding.

_____

_____

_____

_____

_____

_____

_____

_____

_____

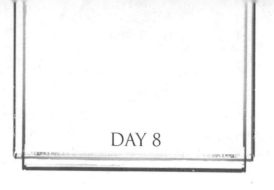

DAY 8

FINDING SECURITY IN GOD'S WORD

All Scripture is inspired by God and is profitable for teaching, for rebuking, for correcting, for training in righteousness, so that the man of God may be complete, equipped for every good work.

—

2 TIMOTHY 3:16-17 HCSB

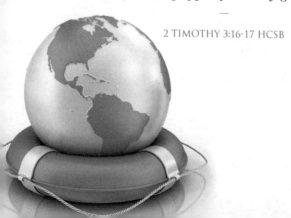

The Bible is God's Word, given to us by God Himself
so we can know Him and His will for our lives.

—

BILLY GRAHAM

The words of Matthew 4:4 remind us that, "Man shall not live by bread alone but by every word that proceedeth out of the mouth of God" (KJV). As believers, we must study the Bible and meditate upon its meaning for our lives. Otherwise, we deprive ourselves of a priceless gift from our Creator.

God's Word is unlike any other book. The Bible is a roadmap for life here on earth and for life eternal. As Christians, we are called upon to study God's Holy Word, to follow its commandments, and to share its Good News with the world.

Jonathan Edwards advised, "Be assiduous in reading the Holy Scriptures. This is the fountain whence all knowledge in divinity must be derived. Therefore let not this treasure lie by you neglected." God's Holy Word is, indeed, a priceless, one-of-a-kind treasure, and a passing acquaintance with the Good Book is insufficient for Christians who seek to obey God's Word and to understand His will. After all, man does not live by bread alone . . .

GOD'S WORD REDUCES STRESS

If you're experiencing stress, God's Word can help relieve it. And if you'd like to experience God's peace, Bible study can help provide it.

Warren Wiersbe observed, "When the child of God looks into the Word of God, he sees the Son of God. And, he is transformed by the Spirit of God to share in the glory of God." God's Holy Word is, indeed, a life-changing, stress-reducing, one-of-a-kind treasure. And it's up to you—and only you—to use it that way.

For as the rain comes down, and the snow from heaven,
and do not return there, but water the earth, and make it
bring forth and bud, that it may give seed to the sower and
bread to the eater, so shall My word be that goes forth
from My mouth; it shall not return to Me void,
but it shall accomplish what I please,
and it shall prosper in the thing for which I sent it.

—

ISAIAH 55:10-11 NKJV

MORE FROM GOD'S WORD ABOUT THE BIBLE

This is my comfort in my affliction, for Your word has given me life.

PSALM 119:50 NKJV

But the word of the Lord endures forever. And this is the word that was preached as the gospel to you.

1 PETER 1:25 HCSB

Let the Word of Christ—the Message—have the run of the house. Give it plenty of room in your lives. Instruct and direct one another using good common sense. And sing, sing your hearts out to God! Let every detail in your lives—words, actions, whatever—be done in the name of the Master, Jesus, thanking God the Father every step of the way.

COLOSSIANS 3:16-17 MSG

For the word of God is living and active. Sharper than any double-edged sword, it penetrates even to dividing soul and spirit, joints and marrow; it judges the thoughts and attitudes of the heart.

HEBREWS 4:12 NIV

MORE POWERFUL IDEAS ABOUT GOD'S WORD

God has given us all sorts of counsel and direction in his written Word; thank God, we have it written down in black and white.

JOHN ELDREDGE

The strength that we claim from God's Word does not depend on circumstances. Circumstances will be difficult, but our strength will be sufficient.

CORRIE TEN BOOM

Nobody ever outgrows Scripture; the book widens and deepens with our years.

C. H. SPURGEON

A TIP FOR TODAY

Take a Bible with you wherever you go. You never know when you may need a midday spiritual pick-me-up.

Prayer and the Word are inseparably linked together. Power in the use of either depends on the presence of the other.

ANDREW MURRAY

A PRAYER FOR TODAY

Heavenly Father, Your Word is a light unto the world; I will study it and trust it and share it. In all that I do, help me be a worthy witness for You as I share the Good News of Your perfect Son and Your perfect Word. Amen

TODAY'S THOUGHTS

My thoughts about the rewards of regular Bible study.

_____

_____

_____

_____

_____

_____

_____

_____

_____

_____

_____

DAY 9

WHEN OLD MAN TROUBLE PAYS A VISIT

When you pass through the waters,
I will be with you; and through the rivers,
they shall not overflow you. When you walk
through the fire, you shall not be burned, nor shall
the flame scorch you. For I am the Lord your God,
The Holy One of Israel, your Savior.

—

ISAIAH 43:2-3 NKJV

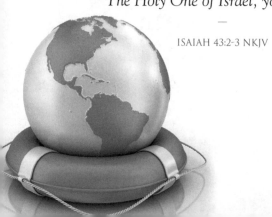

God has given us His promises to assure us and encourage us in the dark days of life.

—

WARREN WIERSBE

As life here on earth unfolds, all of us encounter occasional disappointments and setbacks: those occasional visits from Old Man Trouble are simply a fact of life, and none of us are exempt. When tough times arrive, we may be forced to rearrange our plans and our priorities. But even on our darkest days, we must remember that God's love remains constant.

The fact that we encounter adversity is not nearly so important as the way we choose to deal with it. When tough times arrive, we have a clear choice: we can begin the difficult work of tackling our troubles . . . or not. When we summon the courage to look Old Man Trouble squarely in the eye, he usually blinks. But, if we refuse to address our problems, even the smallest annoyances have a way of growing into king-sized catastrophes.

As believers, we know that God loves us and that He will protect us. In times of hardship, He will comfort us; in times of sorrow, He will dry our tears. When we are troubled, or weak, or sorrowful, God is always with us. We must build our lives on the rock that cannot be shaken: we must trust in God. And then, we must get on with the hard work of tackling our problems . . . because if we don't, who will? Or should?

WHEN YOUR FAITH IS TESTED

Life is a tapestry of good days and difficult days, with good days predominating. During the good days, we are tempted to take our blessings for granted (a temptation that we must resist with all our might). But, during life's difficult days, we discover precisely what we're made of. And more importantly, we discover what our faith is made of.

Has your faith been put to the test yet? If so, then you know that with God's help, you can endure life's darker days. But if you have not yet faced the inevitable trials and tragedies of life here on earth, don't worry: you will. And when your faith is put to the test, rest assured that God is perfectly willing—and always ready—to give you strength for the struggle.

If things are tough, remember that every flower
that ever bloomed had to go through
a whole lot of dirt to get there.

BARBARA JOHNSON

MORE FROM GOD'S WORD ABOUT ADVERSITY

We also have joy with our troubles, because we know that these troubles produce patience. And patience produces character, and character produces hope.

ROMANS 5:3-4 NCV

You pulled me from the brink of death, my feet from the cliff-edge of doom. Now I stroll at leisure with God in the sunlit fields of life.

PSALM 56:13 MSG

Don't fret or worry. Instead of worrying, pray. Let petitions and praises shape your worries into prayers, letting God know your concerns. Before you know it, a sense of God's wholeness, everything coming together for good, will come and settle you down. It's wonderful what happens when Christ displaces worry at the center of your life.

PHILIPPIANS 4:6-7 MSG

Come to Me, all you who labor and are heavy laden, and I will give you rest. Take My yoke upon you and learn from Me, for I am gentle and lowly in heart, and you will find rest for your souls. For My yoke is easy and My burden is light.

MATTHEW 11:28-30 NKJV

MORE POWERFUL IDEAS ABOUT ADVERSITY

A faith that hasn't been tested can't be trusted.

ADRIAN ROGERS

Faith does not eliminate problems. Faith keeps you in a trusting relationship with God in the midst of your problems.

HENRY BLACKABY

I believe that the Creator of this universe takes delight in turning the terrors and tragedies that come with living in this old, fallen domain of the devil and transforming them into something that strengthens our hope, tests our faith, and shows forth His glory.

AL GREEN

A TIP FOR TODAY

If you're having tough times, don't keep everything bottled up inside. Find a person you can really trust, and talk things over.

The happiest people in the world are not those who have no problems, but the people who have learned to live with those things that are less than perfect.

JAMES DOBSON

A PRAYER FOR TODAY

Dear Lord, when I face the inevitable disappointments of life, give me perspective and faith. When I am discouraged, give me the strength to trust Your promises and follow Your will. Then, when I have done my best, Father, let me live with the assurance that You are firmly in control, and that Your love endures forever. Amen

TODAY'S THOUGHTS

My thoughts about some of the lessons I've learned during tough times.

_____

_____

_____

_____

_____

_____

_____

_____

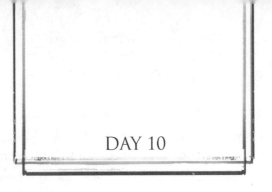

DAY 10

NO PROBLEMS
ARE TOO BIG
FOR GOD

Is anything too hard for the LORD?

—

GENESIS 18:14 KJV

The grace of God is sufficient for all our needs, for every
problem and for every difficulty, for every broken heart,
and for every human sorrow.

—

PETER MARSHALL

Here's a riddle: What is it that is too unimportant
to pray about yet too big for God to handle? The
answer, of course, is: "nothing." Yet sometimes,
when the challenges of the day seem overwhelming, we
may spend more time worrying about our troubles than
praying about them. And, we may spend more time fretting about our problems than solving them. A far better
strategy, of course, is to pray as if everything depended entirely upon God and to work as if everything depended
entirely upon us.

Life is an exercise in problem-solving. The question is
not whether we will encounter problems; the real question
is how we will choose to address them. When it comes to
solving the problems of everyday living, we often know
precisely what needs to be done, but we may be slow in
doing it—especially if what needs to be done is difficult
or uncomfortable for us. So we put off till tomorrow what
should be done today.

The words of Psalm 34 remind us that the Lord solves
problems for "people who do what is right." And usually,

"doing what is right" means doing the uncomfortable work of confronting our problems sooner rather than later. So with no further ado, let the problem-solving begin . . . now!

DO SOMETHING TODAY

Perhaps your troubles are simply too big to solve in a single sitting. But just because you can't solve everything doesn't mean that you should do nothing. So today, as a favor to yourself and as a way of breaking the bonds of procrastination, do something to make your situation better. Even a small step in the right direction is still a step in the right direction. And a small step is far, far better than no step at all.

Be of good courage, and he shall strengthen your heart, all ye that hope in the LORD.

—

PSALM 31:24 KJV

MORE FROM GOD'S WORD ABOUT PROBLEMS

People who do what is right may have many problems, but the Lord will solve them all.

PSALM 34:19 NCV

For when the way is rough, your patience has a chance to grow. So let it grow, and don't try to squirm out of your problems.

JAMES 1:3-4 TLB

When you go through deep waters and great trouble, I will be with you. When you go through the rivers of difficulty, you will not drown! When you walk through the fire of oppression, you will not be burned up; the flames will not consume you. For I am the Lord, your God. . . .

ISAIAH 43:2-3 NLT

Come to me, all you who are weary and burdened, and I will give you rest. Take my yoke upon you and learn from me, for I am gentle and humble in heart, and you will find rest for your souls. For my yoke is easy and my burden is light.

MATTHEW 11:28-30 NIV

MORE POWERFUL IDEAS ABOUT PROBLEMS

Suffering will be either your master or your servant, depending on how you handle the crises of life.

WARREN WIERSBE

Measure the size of the obstacles against the size of God.

BETH MOORE

We must face today as children of tomorrow. We must meet the uncertainties of this world with the certainty of the world to come. To the pure in heart nothing really bad can happen . . . not death, but sin, should be our greatest fear.

A. W. TOZER

A TIP FOR TODAY

When it comes to solving problems, work beats worry. Remember: it is better to fix than to fret.

Troubles we bear trustfully can bring us a fresh vision of God and a new outlook on life, an outlook of peace and hope.

BILLY GRAHAM

A PRAYER FOR TODAY

Lord, sometimes my problems are simply too big for me, but they are never too big for You. Let me turn my troubles over to You, Lord, and let me trust in You today and for all eternity. Amen

TODAY'S THOUGHTS

My thoughts about God's love and about His ability to protect me during difficult times.

_____

_____

_____

_____

_____

_____

_____

_____

_____

DAY 11

TOUGH TIMES BUILD CHARACTER

*People with integrity have firm footing,
but those who follow crooked paths
will slip and fall.*

PROVERBS 10:9 NLT

Character is both developed and revealed by tests,
and all of life is a test.

—

RICK WARREN

Psalm 145 promises, "The Lord is near to all who call
on him, to all who call on him in truth. He fulfills
the desires of those who fear him; he hears their cry
and saves them" (vv. 18-20 NIV). And the words of Jesus
offer us comfort: "These things I have spoken to you, that
in Me you may have peace. In the world you will have tribulation; but be of good cheer, I have overcome the world"
(John 16:33 NKJV).

The times that try your soul are also the times that
build your character. During the darker days of life, you
can learn lessons that are impossible to learn during sun-
ny, happier days. Times of adversity can—and should—be
times of intense spiritual and personal growth. But God
will not force you to learn the lessons of adversity. You
must learn them for yourself.

DO THE HARD THING FIRST

The habit of putting things off until the last minute, along
with its first cousin, the habit of making excuses for work

that was never done, can be detrimental to your life and to your character.

Are you in the habit of doing what needs to be done when it needs to be done, or are you a dues-paying member of the Procrastinator's Club? If you've acquired the habit of doing things sooner rather than later, congratulations! But, if you find yourself putting off all those unpleasant tasks until later (or never), it's time to think about the consequences of your behavior.

One way that you can learn to defeat procrastination is by paying less attention to your fears and more attention to your responsibilities. So, when you're faced with a difficult choice or an unpleasant responsibility, don't spend endless hours fretting over your fate. Simply seek God's counsel and get busy. When you do, you will be richly rewarded because of your willingness to act.

MORE FROM GOD'S WORD ABOUT
CHARACTER

Do not be misled: "Bad company corrupts good character."

1 CORINTHIANS 15:33 NIV

Applying all diligence, in your faith supply moral excellence.

2 PETER 1:5 NASB

The righteousness of the blameless clears his path, but the wicked person will fall because of his wickedness.

PROVERBS 11:5 HCSB

A good name is more desirable than great riches; to be esteemed is better than silver or gold.

PROVERBS 22:1 NIV

We also have joy with our troubles, because we know that these troubles produce patience. And patience produces character, and character produces hope.

ROMANS 5:3-4 NCV

MORE POWERFUL IDEAS ABOUT CHARACTER

Every time you refuse to face up to life and its problems, you weaken your character.

E. STANLEY JONES

Character cannot be developed in ease and quiet. Only through experience of trial and suffering can the soul be strengthened, vision cleared, ambition inspired, and success achieved.

HELEN KELLER

Character is what you are in the dark.

D. L. MOODY

A TIP FOR TODAY

Your challenge is to believe in yourself, to trust God, and to follow God's lead, even if He leads you outside your comfort zone.

Let God use times of waiting to mold and shape your character. Let God use those times to purify your life and make you into a clean vessel for His service.

HENRY BLACKABY AND
CLAUDE KING

76

A PRAYER FOR TODAY

Dear Lord, every day can be an exercise in character-building, and that's what I intend to make this day. I will be mindful that my thoughts and actions have great consequences, consequences in my own life and in the lives of my loved ones. I will strive to make my thoughts and actions pleasing to You, so that I may be an instrument of Your peace, today and every day. Amen

TODAY'S THOUGHTS

My thoughts about the rewards of being truthful and trustworthy.

_____

_____

_____

_____

_____

_____

_____

_____

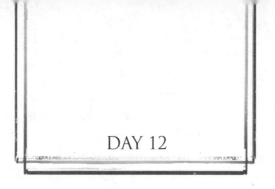

DAY 12

EMBRACING CHANGE

His message was simple and austere,
like his desert surroundings:
"Change your life. God's kingdom is here."
—

MATTHEW 3:2 MSG

Resistance to change is universal.
It invades all classes and cultures.
There is nothing more difficult to undertake or
more uncertain in its success,
than introducing change.

—

JOHN MAXWELL

In our fast-paced world, everyday life has become an exercise in managing change. Our circumstances change; our relationships change; our bodies change. We grow older every day, as does our world. Thankfully, God does not change. He is eternal, as are the truths that are found in His Holy Word.

The ideas in this book are intended to help you accept change—and embrace it—as you continue to seek God's unfolding plan for your life.

Are you facing one of life's inevitable "mid-course corrections"? If so, you must place your faith, your trust, and your life in the hands of the One who does not change: your Heavenly Father. He is the unmoving rock upon which you must construct this day and every day. When you do, you are secure.

ANTICIPATING YOUR NEXT
GRAND ADVENTURE

It has been said that a rut is nothing more than a grave with both ends kicked out. That's a thought worth pondering. Have you made your life an exciting adventure, or have you allowed the distractions of everyday life to rob you of a sense of God's purpose?

As a believing Christian, you have every reason to celebrate. So if you find yourself feeling as if you're stuck in a rut, or in an unfortunate circumstance, or in a difficult relationship, abandon the status quo by making the changes that your heart tells you are right. After all, in God's glorious kingdom, there should be no place for disciples who are dejected, discouraged, or disheartened. God has a far better plan than that, and so should you.

With God, it isn't who you were that matters;
it's who you are becoming.

—

LIZ CURTIS HIGGS

MORE FROM GOD'S WORD ABOUT TRUST

Trust in the Lord with all your heart, and do not rely on your own understanding; think about Him in all your ways, and He will guide you on the right paths.

PROVERBS 3:5-6 HCSB

Let us hold fast the confession of our hope without wavering, for He who promised is faithful.

HEBREWS 10:23 NKJV

For we walk by faith, not by sight.

2 CORINTHIANS 5:7 NKJV

The one who understands a matter finds success, and the one who trusts in the Lord will be happy.

PROVERBS 16:20 HCSB

For the eyes of the Lord range throughout the earth to show Himself strong for those whose hearts are completely His.

2 CHRONICLES 16:9 HCSB

MORE POWERFUL IDEAS ABOUT CHANGE

More often than not, when something looks like it's the absolute end, it is really the beginning.

CHARLES SWINDOLL

In a world kept chaotic by change, you will eventually discover, as I have, that this is one of the most precious qualities of the God we are looking for: He doesn't change.

BILL HYBELS

Mere change is not growth. Growth is the synthesis of change and continuity, and where there is no continuity there is no growth.

C. S. LEWIS

A TIP FOR TODAY

Change is inevitable. Don't fear it. Embrace it.

The secret of contentment in the midst of change is found in having roots in the changeless Christ—the same yesterday, today and forever.

ED YOUNG

A PRAYER FOR TODAY

Dear Lord, our world is constantly changing. When I face the inevitable transitions of life, I will turn to You for strength and assurance. Thank You, Father, for love that is unchanging and everlasting. Amen

TODAY'S THOUGHTS

My thoughts about the need to embrace the changes that God has placed along my path.

_____

_____

_____

_____

_____

_____

_____

_____

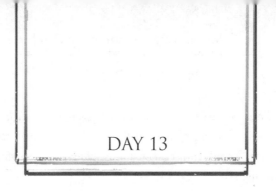

DAY 13

DEFEATING
PROCRASTINATION

*If you wait for perfect conditions,
you will never get anything done.*

—

ECCLESIASTES 11:4 NLT

Not now becomes never.

—

MARTIN LUTHER

When tough times arrive, it's easy (and tempting) to avoid those hard-to-do tasks that you would prefer to avoid altogether. But the habit of procrastination takes a double toll: first, important work goes unfinished, and second, valuable energy is wasted in the process of putting off the things that remain undone.

God has created a world that punishes procrastinators and rewards men and women who "do it now." In other words, life doesn't procrastinate. Neither should you. So if you've been putting things off instead of getting things done, here are some things you can do:

1. Have a clear understanding of your short- and long-term goals, and set your priorities in accordance with those goals.

2. When faced with distasteful tasks, do them immediately, preferably first thing in the morning (even if the unpleasantness is a low-priority activity, go ahead and get it out of the way if it can be completed quickly). Dispatching distasteful tasks sooner rather than later will improve the quality of your day and prevent you from wasting untold amounts of energy in the process of fighting against yourself.

3. Avoid the trap of perfectionism. Be willing to do your best, and be satisfied with the results.

4. If you don't already own one, purchase a daily or weekly planning system that fits your needs. If used properly, a planning calendar is worth many times what you pay for it.

5. Start each work day with a clear written "to-do" list, ranked according to importance. At lunch time, take a moment to collect your thoughts, reexamine your list, and refocus your efforts on the most important things you wish to accomplish during the remainder of the day.

MORE FROM GOD'S WORD ABOUT
PROCRASTINATION

If you do nothing in a difficult time, your strength is limited.

PROVERBS 24:10 HCSB

If you are too lazy to plow in the right season, you will have no food at the harvest.

PROVERBS 20:4 NLT

When you make a vow to God, do not delay in fulfilling it. He has no pleasure in fools; fulfill your vow.

ECCLESIASTES 5:4 NIV

We can't afford to waste a minute, must not squander these precious daylight hours in frivolity and indulgence, in sleeping around and dissipation, in bickering and grabbing everything in sight. Get out of bed and get dressed! Don't loiter and linger, waiting until the very last minute. Dress yourselves in Christ, and be up and about!

ROMANS 13:13-14 MSG

Whatever you do, do it enthusiastically, as something done for the Lord and not for men.

COLOSSIANS 3:23 HCSB

MORE POWERFUL IDEAS ABOUT
PROCRASTINATION

I've found that the worst thing I can do when it comes to any kind of potential pressure situation is to put off dealing with it.

JOHN MAXWELL

Do the unpleasant work first and enjoy the rest of the day.

MARIE T. FREEMAN

Never confuse activity with productivity.

RICK WARREN

A TIP FOR TODAY

The habit of procrastination is often rooted in the fear of failure, the fear of discomfort, or the fear of embarrassment.

Do not build up obstacles in your imagination. Difficulties must be studied and dealt with, but they must not be magnified by fear.

NORMAN VINCENT PEALE

Do noble things, do not dream them all day long.

CHARLES KINGSLEY

A PRAYER FOR TODAY

Dear Lord, when I am confronted with things that need to be done, give me the courage and the wisdom to do them now, not later. Amen

TODAY'S THOUGHTS

My thoughts about important tasks that I have, for now, been postponing.

_____

_____

_____

_____

_____

_____

_____

_____

_____

_____

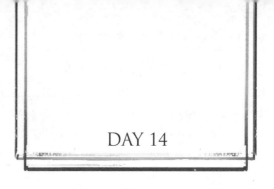

DAY 14

GUARDING YOUR THOUGHTS

Finally brothers, whatever is true, whatever is honorable, whatever is just, whatever is pure, whatever is lovely, whatever is commendable— if there is any moral excellence and if there is any praise—dwell on these things.

—

PHILIPPIANS 4:8 HCSB

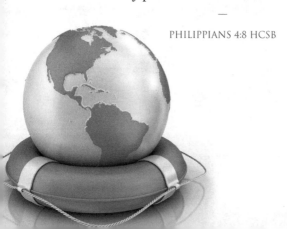

Your thoughts are the determining factor as to whose mold you are conformed to. Control your thoughts and you control the direction of your life.

—

CHARLES STANLEY

Are you an optimistic, hopeful, enthusiastic Christian? You should be. After all, as a believer, you have every reason to be optimistic about life here on earth and life eternal. As English clergyman William Ralph Inge observed, "No Christian should be a pessimist, for Christianity is a system of radical optimism." Inge's words are most certainly true, but sometimes, you may find yourself pulled down by tough times. If you find yourself discouraged, exhausted, or both, then it's time to ask yourself this question: What's bothering you, and why?

If you're worried by the inevitable challenges of everyday living, God wants to have a little talk with you. After all, the ultimate battle has already been won on the cross at Calvary. And if your life has been transformed by Christ's sacrifice, then you, as a recipient of God's grace, have every reason to live courageously.

Are you willing to trust God's plans for your life, in good times and hard times? Hopefully, you will trust Him completely. Proverbs 3:5-6 makes it clear: "Trust in the Lord with all your heart, and lean not on your own understanding; in all your ways acknowledge Him, and He shall direct your paths" (NKJV).

A. W. Tozer noted, "Attitude is all-important. Let the soul take a quiet attitude of faith and love toward God, and from there on, the responsibility is God's. He will make good on His commitments." These words should serve as a reminder that even when the challenges of the day seem daunting, God remains steadfast. And, so should you.

So make this promise to yourself and keep it—vow to be a hope-filled Christian. Think optimistically about your life, your profession, your family, your future, and your purpose for living. Trust your hopes, not your fears. Take time to celebrate God's glorious creation. And then, when you've filled your heart with hope and gladness, share your optimism with others. They'll be better for it, and so will you.

So prepare your minds for service and have self-control.

—

1 PETER 1:13 NCV

MORE FROM GOD'S WORD ABOUT
YOUR THOUGHTS

Come near to God, and God will come near to you. You sinners, clean sin out of your lives. You who are trying to follow God and the world at the same time, make your thinking pure.

JAMES 4:8 NCV

Those who are pure in their thinking are happy, because they will be with God.

MATTHEW 5:8 NCV

Do not conform any longer to the pattern of this world, but be transformed by the renewing of your mind. Then you will be able to test and approve what God's will is—his good, pleasing and perfect will.

ROMANS 12:2 NIV

Dear friend, guard Clear Thinking and Common Sense with your life; don't for a minute lose sight of them. They'll keep your soul alive and well, they'll keep you fit and attractive.

PROVERBS 3:21-22 MSG

MORE POWERFUL IDEAS ABOUT YOUR THOUGHTS

The things we think are the things that feed our souls. If we think on pure and lovely things, we shall grow pure and lovely like them; and the converse is equally true.

HANNAH WHITALL SMITH

It is the thoughts and intents of the heart that shape a person's life.

JOHN ELDREDGE

Attitude is the mind's paintbrush; it can color any situation.

BARBARA JOHNSON

A TIP FOR TODAY

Be a realistic optimist. Think realistically about yourself and your situation while making an effort to focus on hopes, not fears.

I became aware of one very important concept I had missed before: my attitude—not my circumstances—was what was making me unhappy.

VONETTE BRIGHT

A PRAYER FOR TODAY

Dear Lord, I will focus on Your love, Your power, Your promises, and Your Son. When I am weak, I will turn to You for strength; when I am worried, I will turn to You for comfort; when I am troubled, I will turn to You for patience and perspective. Help me guard my thoughts, Lord, so that I may honor You this day and forever. Amen

TODAY'S THOUGHTS

My thoughts about the rewards of focusing on the positive aspects of my life, not the negative ones.

_____

_____

_____

_____

_____

_____

_____

_____

DAY 15

THE LESSONS OF
ADVERSITY

*He heals the brokenhearted and
bandages their wounds.*

—

PSALM 147:3 NCV

> God allows us to experience the low points of life
> in order to teach us lessons that we could
> learn in no other way.
>
> —
>
> C. S. LEWIS

Whether you're twenty-two or a hundred and two, you've still got lots to learn. Even if you're very wise, God isn't finished with you yet, and He isn't finished teaching you important lessons about life here on earth and life eternal.

God does not intend for you to remain stuck in one place. Far from it! God wants you to continue growing as a person and as a Christian every day that you live. And make no mistake: both spiritual and intellectual growth are possible during every stage of life—during the happiest days or the hardest ones.

How can you make sure that you'll keep growing (and learning) during good times and hard times. You do so through prayer, through worship, through fellowship, through an openness to God's Holy Spirit, and through a careful study of God's Holy Word.

Your Bible contains powerful prescriptions for overcoming tough times. When you study God's Word and live according to His commandments, adversity becomes a practical instructor. While you're enduring difficult days, you learn lessons you simply could not have learned any other way. And when you learn those lessons, you will serve as a shining example to your friends, to your family, and to the world.

OLD MAN TROUBLE HAS LESSONS TO TEACH

The next time Old Man Trouble knocks on your door, remember that he has lessons to teach. So turn away Mr. Trouble as quickly as you can, but as you're doing so, don't forget to learn his lessons. And remember: the trouble with trouble isn't just the trouble it causes; it's also the trouble we cause ourselves if we ignore the things that trouble has to teach. Got that? Then please don't forget it!

God's curriculum for all who sincerely want
to know Him and do His will always includes lessons
we wish we could skip. With an intimate understanding
of our deepest needs and individual capacities,
He chooses our curriculum.

—

ELISABETH ELLIOT

MORE FROM GOD'S WORD ABOUT WISDOM

The Lord says, "I will make you wise and show you where to go. I will guide you and watch over you."

PSALM 32:8 NCV

Wisdom is the principal thing; therefore get wisdom. And in all your getting, get understanding.

PROVERBS 4:7 NKJV

Happy is the person who finds wisdom, the one who gets understanding.

PROVERBS 3:13 NCV

Anyone who listens to my teaching and obeys me is wise, like a person who builds a house on solid rock. Though the rain comes in torrents and the floodwaters rise and the winds beat against that house, it won't collapse, because it is built on rock.

MATTHEW 7:24-25 NLT

But the wisdom that is from above is first pure, then peaceable, gentle, willing to yield, full of mercy and good fruits, without partiality and without hypocrisy.

JAMES 3:17 NKJV

MORE POWERFUL IDEAS ABOUT WISDOM

What lessons about honor did you learn from your childhood? Are you living what you learned today?

DENNIS SWANBERG

If your every human plan and calculation has miscarried, if, one by one, human props have been knocked out, take heart. God is trying to get a message through to you, and the message is: "Stop depending on inadequate human resources. Let me handle the matter."

CATHERINE MARSHALL

Life is literally filled with God-appointed storms. These squalls surge across everyone's horizon. We all need them.

CHARLES SWINDOLL

A TIP FOR TODAY

A positive attitude makes a big differ-ence in the way you tackle your problems.

While chastening is always difficult, if we look to God for the lesson we should learn, we will see spiritual fruit.

VONETTE BRIGHT

A PRAYER FOR TODAY

Dear Lord, I have so much to learn. Help me to watch, to listen, to think, and to learn, every day of my life. Amen

TODAY'S THOUGHTS

My thoughts about some of the most important lessons I've learned from tough times.

_____

_____

_____

_____

_____

_____

_____

_____

_____

_____

_____

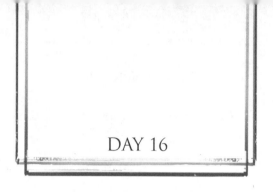

DAY 16

STRENGTH RENEWED

*I will give you a new heart and
put a new spirit within you.*

—

EZEKIEL 36:26 HCSB

Walking with God leads to receiving His intimate counsel, and counseling leads to deep restoration.

—

JOHN ELDREDGE

On occasion, the demands of daily life can drain us of our strength and rob us of the joy that is rightfully ours in Christ. When we find ourselves tired, discouraged, or worse, there is a source from which we can draw the power needed to recharge our spiritual batteries. That source is God.

Is your spiritual battery running low? Is your energy on the wane? Are your emotions frayed? If so, it's time to turn your thoughts and your prayers to your Heavenly Father. When you do, He will provide for your needs, and He will restore your soul.

UNDERSTANDING DEPRESSION

Throughout our lives, all of us must endure personal losses that leave us struggling to find hope. The sadness that accompanies such losses is an inescapable fact of life—but in time, we move beyond our grief as the sadness runs its course and life returns to normal. Depression, however, is more than sadness . . . much more.

Depression is a physical and emotional condition that is, in almost all cases, treatable with medication and counseling. And it is not a disease to be taken lightly. Left untreated, depression presents real dangers to patients' physical health and to their emotional well-being.

If you're feeling blue, perhaps it's a logical response to the disappointments of everyday life. But if your feelings of sadness have lasted longer than you think they should—or if someone close to you fears that your sadness may have evolved into clinical depression—it's time to seek professional help.

Here are a few simple guidelines to consider as you make decisions about possible medical treatment:

1. If your feelings of sadness have resulted in persistent and prolonged changes in sleep patterns, or if you've experienced a significant change in weight (either gain or loss), consult your physician.

2. If you have persistent urges toward self-destructive behavior, or if you feel as though you have lost the will to live, consult a professional counselor or physician immediately.

3. If someone you trust urges you to seek counseling, schedule a session with a professionally trained counselor to evaluate your condition.

4. If you are plagued by consistent, prolonged, severe feelings of hopelessness, consult a physician, a professional counselor, or your pastor.

God's Word has much to say about every aspect of your life, including your emotional health. And, when you face concerns of any sort—including symptoms of depression—remember that God is with you. Your Creator Father intends that His joy should become your joy. Yet sometimes, amid the inevitable hustle and bustle of daily life, you may forfeit—albeit temporarily—God's joy as you wrestle with the challenges of daily living.

So, if you're feeling genuinely depressed, trust your medical doctor to do his or her part. Then, place your ultimate trust in your benevolent Heavenly Father. His healing touch, like His love, endures forever.

By the reading of Scripture I am so renewed that
all nature seems renewed around me and with me.

—

THOMAS MERTON

MORE FROM GOD'S WORD ABOUT RENEWAL

The One who was sitting on the throne said, "Look! I am making everything new!" Then he said, "Write this, because these words are true and can be trusted."

REVELATION 21:5 NCV

Create in me a pure heart, O God, and renew a steadfast spirit within me. Do not cast me from your presence or take your Holy Spirit from me. Restore to me the joy of your salvation and grant me a willing spirit, to sustain me.

PSALM 51:10-12 NIV

He makes me to lie down in green pastures; He leads me beside the still waters. He restores my soul; He leads me in the paths of righteousness for His name's sake.

PSALM 23:2-3 NKJV

Come to Me, all you who labor and are heavy laden, and I will give you rest. Take My yoke upon you and learn from Me, for I am gentle and lowly in heart, and you will find rest for your souls. For My yoke is easy and My burden is light.

MATTHEW 11:28-30 NKJV

MORE POWERFUL IDEAS ABOUT RENEWAL

God is not running an antique shop! He is making all things new!

VANCE HAVNER

No matter how badly we have failed, we can always get up and begin again. Our God is the God of new beginnings.

WARREN WIERSBE

Resolutely slam and lock the door on past sin and failure, and throw away the key.

OSWALD CHAMBERS

God specializes in taking bruised, soiled, broken, guilty, and miserable vessels and making them whole, forgiven, and useful again.

CHARLES SWINDOLL

A TIP FOR TODAY

God wants to give you peace, and He wants to renew your spirit. It's up to you to slow down and give Him a chance to do so.

A PRAYER FOR TODAY

Lord, You are my rock and my strength. When I grow weary, let me turn my thoughts and my prayers to You. When I am discouraged, restore my faith in You. Let me always trust in Your promises, Lord, and let me draw strength from those promises and from Your unending love. Amen

TODAY'S THOUGHTS

My thoughts about God's ability to transform my life and renew my strength.

_____

_____

_____

_____

_____

_____

_____

_____

DAY 17

POWERFUL FAITH PROVIDES THE ULTIMATE SECURITY

*For whatever is born of God overcomes the world.
And this is the victory that has overcome
the world—our faith.*

—

1 JOHN 5:4 NKJV

Only God can move mountains,
but faith and prayer can move God.

—

E. M. BOUNDS

Every life—including yours—is a grand adventure made great by faith. Every step of the way, through every triumph and tragedy, God will stand by your side and strengthen you . . . if you have faith in Him.

Job had every opportunity to give up on himself and to give up on God. But despite his suffering, Job refused to curse his Creator. Job trusted God in the darkest moments of his life, and so did Jesus.

Before His crucifixion, Jesus went to the Mount of Olives and poured out His heart to God (Luke 22). Jesus knew of the agony that He was destined to endure, but He also knew that God's will must be done. We, like our Savior, face trials that bring fear and trembling to the very depths of our souls, but like Jesus, we should seek God's will, not our own.

When you entrust your life to God completely and without reservation, He will give you the strength to meet any challenge, the courage to face any trial, and the wisdom to live in His righteousness and in His peace. So strengthen your faith through praise, through worship, through Bible study, and through prayer. And trust God's plans. With Him, all things are possible, and He stands ready to open a world of possibilities to you . . . if you have faith.

NOURISH YOUR FAITH

When we trust God, we should trust Him without reservation. But sometimes, especially during life's darker days, trusting God may be difficult. Yet this much is certain: whatever our circumstances, we must continue to plant the seeds of faith in our hearts, trusting that in time God will bring forth a bountiful harvest. Planting the seeds for that harvest requires work, which is perfectly okay with God. After all, He never gives us burdens that we cannot bear.

It is important to remember that the work required to build and sustain our faith is an ongoing process. Corrie ten Boom advised, "Be filled with the Holy Spirit; join a church where the members believe the Bible and know the Lord; seek the fellowship of other Christians; learn and be nourished by God's Word and His many promises. Conversion is not the end of your journey—it is only the beginning."

The work of nourishing your faith can and should be joyful work. The hours that you invest in Bible study, prayer, meditation, and worship should be times of enrichment and celebration. And, as you continue to build your life upon a foundation of faith, you will discover that the journey toward spiritual maturity lasts a lifetime. As a child of God, you are never fully "grown": instead, you can continue "growing up" every day of your life. And that's exactly what God wants you to do.

It may be the most difficult time of your life.
You may be enduring your own whirlwind.
But the whirlwind is a temporary experience.
Your faithful, caring Lord will see you through.

—

CHARLES SWINDOLL

MORE FROM GOD'S WORD ABOUT FAITH

Be on the alert, stand firm in the faith, act like men, be strong.

1 CORINTHIANS 16:13 NASB

It is impossible to please God apart from faith. And why? Because anyone who wants to approach God must believe both that he exists and that he cares enough to respond to those who seek him.

HEBREWS 11:6 MSG

Fight the good fight of faith; take hold of the eternal life to which you were called. . . .

1 TIMOTHY 6:12 NASB

Therefore, being always of good courage . . . we walk by faith, not by sight.

2 CORINTHIANS 5:6-7 NASB

I have fought the good fight, I have finished the race, I have kept the faith.

2 TIMOTHY 4:7 NIV

MORE POWERFUL IDEAS ABOUT FAITH

I am truly grateful that faith enables me to move past the question of "Why?"

ZIG ZIGLAR

When you enroll in the "school of faith," you never know what may happen next. The life of faith presents challenges that keep you going—and keep you growing!

WARREN WIERSBE

Nothing is more disastrous than to study faith, analyze faith, make noble resolves of faith, but never actually to make the leap of faith.

VANCE HAVNER

A TIP FOR TODAY

When you have a choice between trusting your feelings or trusting God, trust God. If your faith is strong enough, you and God can move mountains.

Trials are not enemies of faith but opportunities to reveal God's faithfulness.

BARBARA JOHNSON

A PRAYER FOR TODAY

Lord, sometimes this world is a terrifying place. When I am filled with uncertainty and doubt, give me faith. In life's dark moments, help me remember that You are always near and that You can overcome any challenge. Today, Lord, and forever, I will place my trust in You. Amen

TODAY'S THOUGHTS

My thoughts about the power of faith and the certainty of God's promises.

_____

_____

_____

_____

_____

_____

_____

_____

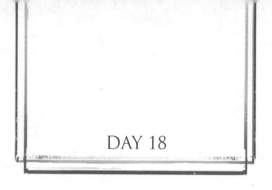

DAY 18

THE RIGHT KIND OF ATTITUDE

*For God has not given us a spirit of fearfulness,
but one of power, love, and sound judgment.*

—

2 TIMOTHY 1:7 HCSB

We are either the masters or the victims of our attitudes.
It is a matter of personal choice. Who we are today is
the result of choices we made yesterday.
Tomorrow, we will become what we choose today.
To change means to choose to change.

—

JOHN MAXWELL

If you want to defeat Old Man Trouble, you'll need the right kind of attitude: the positive kind. So what's your attitude today? Are you fearful, angry, bored, or worried? Are you pessimistic, perplexed, pained, and perturbed? Are you moping around with a frown on your face that's almost as big as the one in your heart? If so, God wants to have a little talk with you.

God created you in His own image, and He wants you to experience joy, contentment, peace, and abundance. But, God will not force you to experience these things; you must claim them for yourself.

God has given you free will, including the ability to influence the direction and the tone of your thoughts. And, here's how God wants you to direct those thoughts:

Finally brothers, whatever is true, whatever is honorable, whatever is just, whatever is pure, whatever is lovely, whatever is commendable—if there is any

moral excellence and if there is any praise—dwell on these things." Philippians 4:8 HCSB

The quality of your attitude will help determine the quality of your life, so you must guard your thoughts accordingly. If you make up your mind to approach life with a healthy mixture of realism and optimism, you'll be rewarded. But, if you allow yourself to fall into the unfortunate habit of negative thinking, you will doom yourself to unhappiness, or mediocrity, or worse.

So, the next time you find yourself dwelling upon the negative aspects of your life, refocus your attention on things positive. The next time you find yourself falling prey to the blight of pessimism, stop yourself and turn your thoughts around. The next time you're tempted to waste valuable time gossiping or complaining, resist those temptations with all your might. And remember: you'll never whine your way to the top . . . so don't waste your breath.

MORE FROM GOD'S WORD ABOUT
YOUR ATTITUDE

Set your mind on things above, not on things on the earth.

COLOSSIANS 3:2 NKJV

Come near to God, and God will come near to you. You sinners, clean sin out of your lives. You who are trying to follow God and the world at the same time, make your thinking pure.

JAMES 4:8 NCV

Those who are pure in their thinking are happy, because they will be with God.

MATTHEW 5:8 NCV

Your attitude should be the same as that of Christ Jesus: Who, being in very nature God, did not consider equality with God something to be grasped, but made himself nothing, taking the very nature of a servant, being made in human likeness. And being found in appearance as a man, he humbled himself and became obedient to death—even death on a cross!

PHILIPPIANS 2:5-8 NIV

So prepare your minds for service and have self-control.

1 PETER 1:13 NCV

119

MORE POWERFUL IDEAS ABOUT YOUR ATTITUDE

We shouldn't deny the pain of what happens in our lives. But, we should refuse to focus only on the valleys.

CHARLES SWINDOLL

Attitude is more important than the past, than education, than money, than circumstances, than what people do or say. It is more important than appearance, giftedness, or skill.

CHARLES SWINDOLL

The mind is like a clock that is constantly running down. It has to be wound up daily with good thoughts.

FULTON J. SHEEN

A TIP FOR TODAY

A positive attitude leads to positive results; a negative attitude leads elsewhere. If you want to improve the quality of your thoughts, ask God to help you.

The difference between winning and losing is how we choose to react to disappointment.

BARBARA JOHNSON

A PRAYER FOR TODAY

Lord, I pray for an attitude that is Christlike. Whatever my circumstances, whether good or bad, triumphal or tragic, let my response reflect a God-honoring attitude of optimism, faith, and love for You. Amen

TODAY'S THOUGHTS

My thoughts about the importance of maintaining a positive attitude during challenging times.

_____

_____

_____

_____

_____

_____

_____

_____

_____

DAY 19

TRUSTING
GOD'S TIMING

*I waited patiently for the LORD;
and He inclined to me, and heard my cry.*

—

PSALM 40:1 NKJV

Will not the Lord's time be better than your time?

—

C. H. SPURGEON

The Bible teaches us to trust God's timing in all matters, but we are sorely tempted to do otherwise, especially when times are tough. When we are beset with problems, we are understandably anxious for a quick conclusion to our hardships. We know that our problems will end some day, and we want it to end NOW. God, however, works on His own timetable, and His schedule does not always coincide with ours.

God's plans are perfect; ours most certainly are not. So we must learn to trust the Father in good times and hard times. No exceptions.

Elisabeth Elliot advised, "We must learn to move according to the timetable of the Timeless One, and to be at peace." And Billy Graham observed, "As we wait on God, He helps us use the winds of adversity to soar above our problems."

So today, as you meet the challenges of everyday life, do your best to turn everything over to God. Whatever "it" is, He can handle it. And you can be sure that He will handle it when the time is right.

PRAY FOR PATIENCE

Would you like to become a more patient person? Pray about it. Is there a person you dislike? Pray for a forgiving heart. Do you lose your temper more than you should? Ask God for help. Are you mired in the quicksand of regret? Ask God to liberate you.

As you pray more, you'll discover that God is always near and that He's always ready to hear from you. So don't worry about things; pray about them. God is waiting . . . and listening!

> When life is difficult, God wants us
> to have a faith that trusts and waits.
>
> —
>
> KAY ARTHUR

MORE FROM GOD'S WORD ABOUT
HIS TIMING

Humble yourselves, therefore, under God's mighty hand, that he may lift you up in due time.

1 PETER 5:6 NIV

He told them, "You don't get to know the time. Timing is the Father's business."

ACTS 1:7 MSG

From one man he made every nation of men, that they should inhabit the whole earth; and he determined the times set for them and the exact places where they should live.

ACTS 17:26 NIV

There is a time for everything, and a season for every activity under heaven.

ECCLESIASTES 3:1 NIV

Yet the LORD longs to be gracious to you; he rises to show you compassion. For the LORD is a God of justice. Blessed are all who wait for him!

ISAIAH 30:18 NIV

MORE POWERFUL IDEAS ABOUT GOD'S TIMING

By his wisdom, he orders his delays so that they prove to be far better than our hurries.

C. H. SPURGEON

Waiting on God brings us to the journey's end quicker than our feet.

MRS. CHARLES E. COWMAN

When we read of the great Biblical leaders, we see that it was not uncommon for God to ask them to wait, not just a day or two, but for years, until God was ready for them to act.

GLORIA GAITHER

A TIP FOR TODAY

God is in control of His world and your world. Rely upon Him.

Our challenge is to wait in faith for the day of God's favor and salvation.

JIM CYMBALA

A PRAYER FOR TODAY

Dear Lord, Your timing is seldom my timing, but Your timing is always right for me. You are my Father, and You have a plan for my life that is grander than I can imagine. When I am impatient, remind me that You are never early or late. You are always on time, Lord, so let me trust in You . . . always. Amen

TODAY'S THOUGHTS

My thoughts about the need to trust God in all matters, including the time in which He chooses to reveal His plans and purposes.

DAY 20

ASK HIM

*So I say to you, keep asking, and it will be given
to you. Keep searching, and you will find.
Keep knocking, and the door will be opened to you.*

—

LUKE 11:9 HCSB

God will help us become the people we are
meant to be, if only we will ask Him.

—

HANNAH WHITALL SMITH

How often do you ask God for His help and His wisdom? Occasionally? Intermittently? Whenever you experience a crisis? Hopefully not. Hopefully, you've acquired the habit of asking for God's assistance early and often. And hopefully, you have learned to seek His guidance in every aspect of your life.

Jesus made it clear to His disciples: they should petition God to meet their needs. So should you. Genuine, heartfelt prayer produces powerful changes in you and in your world. When you lift your heart to God, you open yourself to a never-ending source of divine wisdom and infinite love.

James 5:16 makes a promise that God intends to keep: when you pray earnestly, fervently, and often, great things will happen. Too many people, however, are too timid or too pessimistic to ask God to do big things. Please don't count yourself among their number.

God can do great things through you if you have the courage to ask Him (and the determination to keep asking Him). But don't expect Him to do all the work. When you

129

do your part, He will do His part—and when He does, you can expect miracles to happen.

The Bible promises that God will guide you if you let Him. Your job is to let Him. But sometimes, you will be tempted to do otherwise. Sometimes, you'll be tempted to go along with the crowd; other times, you'll be tempted to do things your way, not God's way. When you feel those temptations, resist them.

God has promised that when you ask for His help, He will not withhold it. So ask. Ask Him to meet the needs of your day. Ask Him to lead you, to protect you, and to correct you. Then, trust the answers He gives.

God stands at the door and waits. When you knock, He opens. When you ask, He answers. Your task, of course, is to make God a full partner in every aspect of your life— in good times and in hard times—and to seek His guidance prayerfully, confidently, and often.

Until now you have not asked for anything in my name.
Ask and you will receive,
so that your joy will be the fullest possible joy.

—

JOHN 16:24 NCV

130

MORE FROM GOD'S WORD ABOUT ASKING HIM FOR THE THINGS YOU NEED

If you need wisdom—if you want to know what God wants you to do—ask him, and he will gladly tell you. He will not resent your asking.

JAMES 1:5 NLT

From now on, whatever you request along the lines of who I am and what I am doing, I'll do it. That's how the Father will be seen for who he is in the Son. I mean it. Whatever you request in this way, I'll do.

JOHN 14:13-14 MSG

You did not choose me, but I chose you and appointed you to go and bear fruit—fruit that will last. Then the Father will give you whatever you ask in my name.

JOHN 15:16 NIV

You fathers—if your children ask for a fish, do you give them a snake instead? Or if they ask for an egg, do you give them a scorpion? Of course not! If you sinful people know how to give good gifts to your children, how much more will your heavenly Father give the Holy Spirit to those who ask him.

LUKE 11:11-13 NLT

131

MORE POWERFUL IDEAS ABOUT ASKING GOD

We sometimes fear to bring our troubles to God, because they must seem so small to him who sitteth on the circle of the earth. But, if they are large enough to vex and endanger our welfare, they are large enough to touch his heart of love.

R. A. TORREY

When will we realize that we're not troubling God with our questions and concerns? His heart is open to hear us—his touch nearer than our next thought—as if no one in the world existed but us. Our very personal God wants to hear from us personally.

GIGI GRAHAM TCHIVIDJIAN

A TIP FOR TODAY

When you ask God for His assistance, He hears your request—and in His own time, He answers. If you need more, ask more.

Don't be afraid to ask your heavenly Father for anything you need. Indeed, nothing is too small for God's attention or too great for his power.

DENNIS SWANBERG

A PRAYER FOR TODAY

Dear Lord, when I have questions or fears, I will turn to You. When I am weak, I will seek Your strength. When I am discouraged, Father, I will be mindful of Your love and Your grace. I will ask You for the things I need, Father, and I will trust Your answers, today and forever. Amen

TODAY'S THOUGHTS

My thoughts about the things I need to ask God for today.

_____

_____

_____

_____

_____

_____

_____

_____

_____

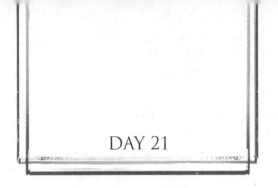

DAY 21

WISDOM PROTECTS

Acquire wisdom—how much better it is than gold!
And acquire understanding—
it is preferable to silver.

PROVERBS 16:16 HCSB

Wise people listen to wise instruction, especially instruction from the Word of God.

—

WARREN WIERSBE

D o you place a high value on the acquisition of wisdom? If so, you are not alone; most people would like to be wise, but not everyone is willing to do the work that is required to become wise. Wisdom is not like a mushroom; it does not spring up overnight. It is, instead, like an oak tree that starts as a tiny acorn, grows into a sapling, and eventually reaches up to the sky, tall and strong.

To become wise, you must seek God's guidance and live according to His Word. To become wise, you must seek instruction with consistency and purpose. To become wise, you must not only learn the lessons of the Christian life, but you must also live by them. But oftentimes, that's easier said than done.

Sometimes, amid the demands of daily life, you will lose perspective. Life may seem out of balance, and the pressures of everyday living may seem overwhelming. What's needed is a fresh perspective, a restored sense of balance . . . and God's wisdom. If you call upon the Lord and seek to see the world through His eyes, He will give you guidance, wisdom, and perspective. When you make

God's priorities your priorities, He will lead you according to His plan and according to His commandments. When you study God's teachings, you are reminded that God's reality is the ultimate reality.

Do you seek to live a life of righteousness and wisdom? If so, you must study the ultimate source of wisdom: the Word of God. You must seek out worthy mentors and listen carefully to their advice. You must associate, day in and day out, with godly men and women. Then, as you accumulate wisdom, you must not keep it for yourself; you must, instead, share it with your friends and family members.

But be forewarned: if you sincerely seek to share your hard-earned wisdom with others, your actions must reflect the values that you hold dear. The best way to share your wisdom—perhaps the only way—is not by your words, but by your example.

A wise man will hear and increase learning,
and a man of understanding will attain wise counsel.

—

PROVERBS 1:5 NKJV

MORE FROM GOD'S WORD ABOUT
HIS WISDOM

The fear of the Lord is the beginning of wisdom; a good understanding have all those who do His commandments. His praise endures forever.

PSALM 111:10 NKJV

So teach us to number our days, that we may gain a heart of wisdom.

PSALM 90:12 NKJV

Teach me, O Lord, the way of Your statutes, and I shall keep it to the end.

PSALM 119:33 NKJV

Therefore, everyone who hears these words of Mine and acts on them will be like a sensible man who built his house on the rock. The rain fell, the rivers rose, and the winds blew and pounded that house. Yet it didn't collapse, because its foundation was on the rock.

MATTHEW 7:24-25 HCSB

137

MORE POWERFUL IDEAS ABOUT WISDOM

If you lack knowledge, go to school. If you lack wisdom, get on your knees.

VANCE HAVNER

Let your old age be childlike, and childhood like old age; that is, so that neither may your wisdom be with pride, nor your humility without wisdom.

ST. AUGUSTINE

The more wisdom enters our hearts, the more we will be able to trust our hearts in difficult situations.

JOHN ELDREDGE

A TIP FOR TODAY

God makes His wisdom available to you. Your job is to acknowledge, to understand, and (above all) to use that wisdom.

The fruit of wisdom is Christlikeness, peace, humility, and love. And, the root of it is faith in Christ as the manifested wisdom of God.

J. I. PACKER

A PRAYER FOR TODAY

Dear Lord, when I trust in the wisdom of the world, I am often led astray, but when I trust in Your wisdom, I build my life upon a firm foundation. Today and every day I will trust Your Word and follow it, knowing that the ultimate wisdom is Your wisdom and the ultimate truth is Your truth. Amen

TODAY'S THOUGHTS

My thoughts about the rewards of behaving wisely and the dangers of behaving impulsively.

_____

_____

_____

_____

_____

_____

_____

_____

_____

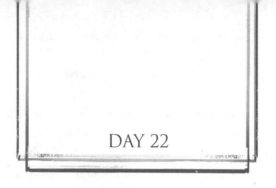

DAY 22

FINDING SECURITY IN THE POWER OF PRAYER

Is anyone among you suffering? He should pray.
Is anyone cheerful? He should sing praises.

—

JAMES 5:13 HCSB

The story of every great Christian achievement is
the history of answered prayer.

—

E. M. BOUNDS

God is trying to get His message through . . . to
you! Are you listening?

Perhaps, if you're experiencing tough times,
you may find yourself overwhelmed by the press of everyday life. Perhaps you forget to slow yourself down long
enough to talk with God. Instead of turning your thoughts
and prayers to Him, you may rely upon our own resources.
Instead of asking God for guidance, you may depend only
upon your own limited wisdom. A far better course of action is this: simply stop what you're doing long enough
to open your heart to God; then listen carefully for His
directions.

Do you spend time each day with God? You should.
Are you in need? Ask God to sustain you. Are you trou-
bled? Take your worries to Him in prayer. Are you weary?
Seek God's strength. In all things great and small, seek
God's wisdom and His grace. He hears your prayers, and
He will answer. All you must do is ask.

GOT QUESTIONS?

You've got questions? God's got answers. And if you'd like to hear from Him, here's precisely what you must do: petition Him with a sincere heart; be still; be patient; and listen. Then, in His own time and in His own fashion, God will answer your questions and give you guidance for the journey ahead.

Today, turn over everything to your Creator. Pray constantly about matters great and small. Seek God's instruction and His direction. And remember: God hears your prayers and answers them. But He won't answer the prayers that you don't get around to praying. So pray early and often. And then wait patiently for answers that are sure to come.

Prayer accomplishes more than anything else.

—

BILL BRIGHT

MORE FROM GOD'S WORD ABOUT PRAYER

"Relax, Daniel," he continued, *"don't be afraid. From the moment you decided to humble yourself to receive understanding, your prayer was heard, and I set out to come to you."*

DANIEL 10:12 MSG

If you don't know what you're doing, pray to the Father. He loves to help. You'll get his help, and won't be condescended to when you ask for it. Ask boldly, believingly, without a second thought. People who "worry their prayers" are like wind-whipped waves. Don't think you're going to get anything from the Master that way, adrift at sea, keeping all your options open.

JAMES 1:5-8 MSG

Rejoice always, pray without ceasing, in everything give thanks; for this is the will of God in Christ Jesus for you.

1 THESSALONIANS 5:16-18 NKJV

I want men everywhere to lift up holy hands in prayer, without anger or disputing.

1 TIMOTHY 2:8 NIV

MORE POWERFUL IDEAS ABOUT PRAYER

God always answers the prayers of His children—but His answer isn't always "Yes."

BILLY GRAHAM

I have found the perfect antidote for fear. Whenever it sticks up its ugly face, I clobber it with prayer.

DALE EVANS ROGERS

Any concern that is too small to be turned into a prayer is too small to be made into a burden.

CORRIE TEN BOOM

A TIP FOR TODAY

We should remember that our prayers are always answered by a loving God, and that we must trust Him, whether He answers "Yes," "No," or "Not yet."

When we pray, we have linked ourselves with Divine purposes, and we therefore have Divine power at our disposal for human living.

E. STANLEY JONES

A PRAYER FOR TODAY

Dear Lord, make me a man of constant prayer. Your Holy Word commands me to pray without ceasing. Let me take everything to You. When I am discouraged, let me pray. When I am lonely, let me take my sorrows to You. When I grieve, let me take my tears to You, Lord, in prayer. And when I am joyful, let me offer up prayers of thanksgiving. In all things great and small, at all times, whether happy or sad, let me seek Your wisdom and Your grace . . . in prayer. Amen

TODAY'S THOUGHTS

My thoughts about the role that prayer does play—and should play—in the way that I meet life's challenges.

_____

_____

_____

_____

_____

_____

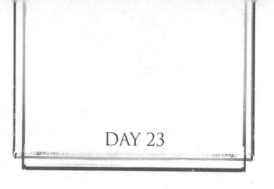

DAY 23

DON'T GIVE UP!

No matter how many times you trip them up,
God-loyal people don't stay down long;
Soon they're up on their feet,
while the wicked end up flat on their faces.

—

PROVERBS 24:16 MSG

We don't give up. We look up. We trust. We believe.
And our optimism is not hollow.
Christ has proven worthy.
He has shown that he never fails.
That's what makes God, God.

—

MAX LUCADO

The old saying is as true today as it was when it was first spoken: "Life is a marathon, not a sprint." That's why wise travelers (like you) select a traveling companion who never tires and never falters. That partner, of course, is your Heavenly Father.

The next time you find your courage tested to the limit, remember that God is as near as your next breath, and remember that He offers strength and comfort to His children. He is your shield and your strength; He is your protector and your deliverer. Call upon Him in your hour of need and then be comforted. Whatever your challenge, whatever your trouble, God can help you persevere. And that's precisely what He'll do if you ask Him.

Perhaps you are in a hurry for God to help you resolve your difficulties. Perhaps you're anxious to earn the rewards that you feel you've already earned from life. Perhaps you're drumming your fingers, impatiently waiting for God to act. If so, be forewarned: God operates on His own timetable, not yours. Sometimes, God may answer your prayers with silence, and when He does, you must patiently persevere. In times of trouble, you must remain steadfast and trust in the merciful goodness of your Heavenly Father. Whatever your problem, He can handle it. Your job is to keep persevering until He does.

HE OVERCOMES THE WORLD

Today he's a respected pastor in Memphis, Tennessee. But in the 1970s, he was just about as far from the church as he could get. As one of the best-selling recording artists in the world, Al Green lived life in the fast lane, and he didn't spend much time thinking or talking about God. But all that changed in 1977 when Green faced personal tragedy that caused him to reassess his life and turn it over to God.

Today, Reverend Al's advice is straightforward. He says, "If you just hang in there with God, everything's gonna be alright."

First John 5:4 tells us, "Whatever is born of God overcomes the world." And that means you. So if Old Man Trouble knocks on your door, remember the words of Reverend Al Green: if you stand with God, He'll stand by you, today, tomorrow, and forever.

148

MORE FROM GOD'S WORD ABOUT PERSEVERANCE

Let us not become weary in doing good, for at the proper time we will reap a harvest if we do not give up.

GALATIANS 6:9 NIV

For you have need of endurance, so that when you have done the will of God, you may receive what was promised.

HEBREWS 10:36 NASB

Thanks be to God! He gives us the victory through our Lord Jesus Christ. Therefore, my dear brothers, stand firm. Let nothing move you. Always give yourselves fully to the work of the Lord, because you know that your labor in the Lord is not in vain.

1 CORINTHIANS 15:57-58 NIV

Be diligent that ye may be found of him in peace, without spot, and blameless.

2 PETER 3:14 KJV

It is better to finish something than to start it. It is better to be patient than to be proud.

ECCLESIASTES 7:8 NCV

MORE POWERFUL IDEAS ABOUT PERSEVERANCE

The sermon of your life in tough times ministers to people more powerfully than the most eloquent speaker.

BILL BRIGHT

Failure is one of life's most powerful teachers. How we handle our failures determines whether we're going to simply "get by" in life or "press on."

BETH MOORE

Just remember, every flower that ever bloomed had to go through a whole lot of dirt to get there!

BARBARA JOHNSON

A TIP FOR TODAY

Whatever your challenge, whatever your trouble, God can give you the strength to persevere, and that's exactly what you should ask Him to do.

When you accept disappointment, when you trust God, and when you yield to Him, you leave something behind to help others in the battles of life.

WARREN WIERSBE

A PRAYER FOR TODAY

Lord, when life is difficult, I am tempted to abandon hope in the future. But You are my God, and I can draw strength from You. Let me trust You, Father, in good times and in bad times. Let me persevere—even if my soul is troubled—and let me follow Your Son, Jesus Christ, this day and forever. Amen

TODAY'S THOUGHTS

My thoughts about the power of perseverance.

_____

_____

_____

_____

_____

_____

_____

_____

_____

_____

DAY 24

LIVE COURAGEOUSLY

They do not fear bad news; they confidently trust the Lord to care for them. They are confident and fearless and can face their foes triumphantly.

—

PSALM 112:7-8 NLT

Faith not only can help you through a crisis, it can help you to approach life after the hard times with a whole new perspective. It can help you adopt an outlook of hope and courage through faith to face reality.

—

JOHN MAXWELL

Every man's life is a tapestry of events: some wonderful, some not-so-wonderful, and some downright disastrous. When we visit the mountaintops of life, praising God isn't hard—in fact, it's easy. In our moments of triumph, we can bow our heads and thank God for our victories. But when we fail to reach the mountaintops, when we endure the inevitable losses that are a part of every person's life, we find it much tougher to give God the praise He deserves. Yet wherever we find ourselves, whether on the mountaintops of life or in life's darkest valleys, we must still offer thanks to God, giving thanks in all circumstances.

The next time you find yourself worried about the challenges of today or the uncertainties of tomorrow, ask yourself this question: Are you really ready to place your concerns and your life in God's all-powerful, all-knowing, all-loving hands? If the answer to that question is yes—as it should be—then you can draw courage today from the source of strength that never fails: your Father in heaven.

God is not a distant being. He is not absent from our world, nor is He absent from your world. God is not "out there"; He is "right here," continuously reshaping His universe, and continuously reshaping the lives of those who dwell in it.

God is with you always, listening to your thoughts and prayers, watching over your every move. If the demands of everyday life weigh down upon you, you may be tempted to ignore God's presence or—worse yet—to lose faith in His promises. But, when you quiet yourself and acknowledge His presence, God will touch your heart and restore your courage.

At this very moment—as you're fulfilling your obligations and overcoming tough times—God is seeking to work in you and through you. He's asking you to live abundantly and courageously . . . and He's ready to help. So why not let Him do it . . . starting now?

Faith is stronger than fear.

—

JOHN MAXWELL

MORE FROM GOD'S WORD ABOUT COURAGE

Be strong and courageous, and do the work. Don't be afraid or discouraged by the size of the task, for the LORD God, my God, is with you. He will not fail you or forsake you.

1 CHRONICLES 28:20 NLT

Therefore, being always of good courage . . . we walk by faith, not by sight.

2 CORINTHIANS 5:6-7 NASB

God doesn't want us to be shy with his gifts, but bold and loving and sensible.

2 TIMOTHY 1:7 MSG

The LORD himself goes before you and will be with you; he will never leave you nor forsake you. Do not be afraid; do not be discouraged.

DEUTERONOMY 31:8 NIV

But Moses said to the people, "Do not fear! Stand by and see the salvation of the LORD."

EXODUS 14:13 NASB

MORE POWERFUL IDEAS ABOUT COURAGE

Seeing that a Pilot steers the ship in which we sail, who will never allow us to perish even in the midst of shipwrecks, there is no reason why our minds should be overwhelmed with fear and overcome with weariness.

JOHN CALVIN

Like dynamite, God's power is only latent power until it is released. You can release God's dynamite power into people's lives and into the world through faith, through words, and through prayer.

BILL BRIGHT

Do not let Satan deceive you into being afraid of God's plans for your life.

R. A. TORREY

A TIP FOR TODAY

With God as your partner, you have nothing to fear. When you sincerely turn to Him, He will never fail you.

Jesus Christ can make the weakest man into a divine dreadnought, fearing nothing.

OSWALD CHAMBERS

156

A PRAYER FOR TODAY

Lord, sometimes I face challenges that leave me breathless. When I am fearful, let me lean upon You. Keep me ever mindful, Lord, that You are my God, my strength, and my shield. With You by my side, I have nothing to fear. And, with Your Son, Jesus, as my Savior, I have received the priceless gift of eternal life. Help me to be a grateful and courageous servant this day and every day. Amen

TODAY'S THOUGHTS

My thoughts about trusting God to lead me through and beyond today's challenges.

_____

_____

_____

_____

_____

_____

_____

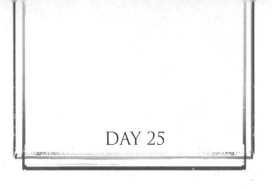

DAY 25

BEWARE OF
THE ADVERSARY

*Therefore, submit to God. But resist the Devil,
and he will flee from you. Draw near to God,
and He will draw near to you. Cleanse your hands,
sinners, and purify your hearts,
double-minded people!*

—

JAMES 4:7-8 HCSB

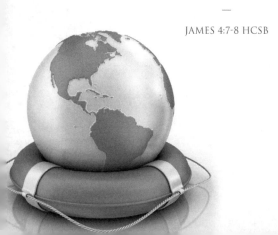

Rebuke the Enemy in your own name and he laughs;
command him in the name of Christ and he flees.

—

JOHN ELDREDGE

This world is God's creation, and it contains the wonderful fruits of His handiwork. But, the world also contains countless opportunities to stray from God's will. Temptations are everywhere, and the devil, it seems, never takes a day off. Our task, as believers, is to turn away from temptation and to place our lives squarely in the center of God's will.

In his letter to Jewish Christians, Peter offered a stern warning: "Your adversary, the devil, prowls around like a roaring lion, seeking someone to devour" (1 Peter 5:8 NASB). What was true in New Testament times is equally true in our own. Evil is indeed abroad in the world, and Satan continues to sow the seeds of destruction far and wide. In a very real sense, our world is at war: good versus evil, sin versus righteousness, hope versus suffering, praise versus apathy. As Christians, we must ensure that we place ourselves squarely on the right side of these conflicts: God's side. How can we do it? By thoughtfully studying God's Word, by regularly worshiping with fellow believers, and by guarding our hearts and minds against the subtle temptations of the enemy. When we do, we are protected.

Are you a man who is determined to stand up against evil whenever and wherever you confront it? And are you fully prepared to distance yourself from the countless temptations that have become so thoroughly woven into the fabric of society? If so, congratulations. That means you're an active-duty participant in the battle against a powerful and dangerous adversary. And with God's help, you're destined to win the battle and the war.

God shapes the world by prayer.
The more praying there is in the world,
the better the world will be, and the mightier
will be the forces against evil.

—

E. M. BOUNDS

MORE FROM GOD'S WORD ABOUT EVIL

Do not be conquered by evil, but conquer evil with good.

ROMANS 12:21 HCSB

For everyone who practices wicked things hates the light and avoids it, so that his deeds may not be exposed. But anyone who lives by the truth comes to the light, so that his works may be shown to be accomplished by God.

JOHN 3:20-21 HCSB

He replied, "Every plant that My heavenly Father didn't plant will be uprooted."

MATTHEW 15:13 HCSB

But the path of the just is like the shining sun, that shines ever brighter unto the perfect day. The way of the wicked is like darkness; they do not know what makes them stumble.

PROVERBS 4:18-19 NKJV

Don't consider yourself to be wise; fear the Lord and turn away from evil.

PROVERBS 3:7 HCSB

MORE POWERFUL IDEAS ABOUT EVIL

Christianity isn't a religion about going to Sunday school, potluck suppers, being nice, holding car washes, sending your secondhand clothes off to Mexico—as good as those things might be. This is a world at war.

JOHN ELDREDGE

God loves you, and He yearns for you to turn away from the path of evil. You need His forgiveness, and you need Him to come into your life and remake you from within.

BILLY GRAHAM

Of two evils, choose neither.

C. H. SPURGEON

A TIP FOR TODAY

Your world is full of distractions and temptations. Your challenge is to live in the world but not be of the world.

The descent to hell is easy, and those who begin by worshipping power soon worship evil.

C. S. LEWIS

162

A PRAYER FOR TODAY

Lord, strengthen my walk with You. Evil comes in many disguises, and sometimes it is only with Your help that I can recognize right from wrong. Your presence in my life enables me to choose truth and to live a life pleasing to You. May I always live in Your presence. Amen

TODAY'S THOUGHTS

My thoughts about the dangerous temptations that face me and my loved ones.

_____

_____

_____

_____

_____

_____

_____

_____

DAY 26

ACCEPTING ADVICE

A wise man will hear and increase learning,
and a man of understanding
will attain wise counsel.

—

PROVERBS 1:5 NKJV

God guides through the counsel of good people.

—

E. STANLEY JONES

If you find yourself caught up in a difficult situation, it's time to start searching for knowledgeable friends and mentors who can give you solid advice. Why do you need help evaluating the person in the mirror? Because you're simply too close to that person, that's why. Sometimes, you'll be tempted to give yourself straight As when you deserve considerably lower grades. On other occasions, you'll become your own worst critic, giving yourself a string of failing marks when you deserve better. The truth, of course, is often somewhere in the middle.

Finding a wise mentor is only half the battle. It takes just as much wisdom—and sometimes more—to act upon good advice as it does to give it. So find people you can trust, listen to them carefully, and act accordingly.

FIND A MENTOR

If you're going through tough times, it's helpful to find mentors who have been there, and done that—people who have experienced your particular challenge and lived to tell about it.

When you find mentors who are godly men and women, you become a more godly person yourself. That's why you should seek out advisors who, by their words and their presence, make you a better person and a better Christian.

Today, as a gift to yourself, select, from your friends and family members a mentor whose judgment you trust. Then listen carefully to your mentor's advice and be willing to accept that advice, even if accepting it requires effort, or pain, or both. Consider your mentor to be God's gift to you. Thank God for that gift, and use it for the glory of His kingdom.

> It takes a wise person to give good advice,
> but an even wiser person to take it.
>
> —
>
> MARIE T. FREEMAN

MORE FROM GOD'S WORD ABOUT ACCEPTING ADVICE

He is God. Let him do whatever he thinks best.

1 SAMUEL 3:18 MSG

It is better to be a poor but wise youth than to be an old and foolish king who refuses all advice.

ECCLESIASTES 4:13 NLT

It is better to listen to rebuke from a wise person than to listen to the song of fools.

ECCLESIASTES 7:5 HCSB

Know-it-alls don't like being told what to do; they avoid the company of wise men and women.

PROVERBS 15:12 MSG

Listen to counsel and receive instruction so that you may be wise in later life.

PROVERBS 19:20 HCSB

MORE POWERFUL IDEAS ABOUT LEARNING FROM OTHER CHRISTIANS

The next best thing to being wise oneself is to live in a circle of those who are.

C. S. LEWIS

The effective mentor strives to help a man or woman discover what they can be in Christ and then holds them accountable to become that person.

HOWARD HENDRICKS

A TIP FOR TODAY

If you can't seem to listen to constructive criticism with an open mind, perhaps you've got a severe case of old-fashioned stubbornness. If so, ask God to soften your heart, open your ears, and enlighten your mind.

God often keeps us on the path by guiding us through the counsel of friends and trusted spiritual advisors.

BILL HYBELS

Do not open your heart to every man, but discuss your affairs with one who is wise and who fears God.

THOMAS À KEMPIS

A PRAYER FOR TODAY

Dear Lord, thank You for the mentors whom You have placed along my path. When I am troubled, let me turn to them for help, for guidance, for comfort, and for perspective. And Father, let me be a friend and mentor to others, so that my love for You may be demonstrated by my genuine concern for them. Amen

TODAY'S THOUGHTS

My thoughts about the wisdom of accepting advice from wise people I trust.

_____

_____

_____

_____

_____

_____

_____

_____

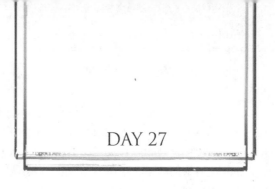

DAY 27

A RENEWED SENSE OF PURPOSE

You will show me the way of life,
granting me the joy of your presence and
the pleasures of living with you forever.

———

PSALM 16:11 NLT

God will make obstacles serve His purpose.

—

MRS. CHARLES E. COWMAN

If you're experiencing tough times, you may be asking yourself, "What does God want me to do next?" Perhaps you're pondering your future, uncertain of your plans, unsure of your next step. But even if you don't have a clear plan for the next step of your life's journey, you may rest assured that God does.

God has a plan for the universe, and He has a plan for you. He understands that plan as thoroughly and completely as He knows you. If you seek God's will earnestly and prayerfully, He will make His plans known to you in His own time and in His own way.

Do you sincerely want to discover God's purpose for your life? If so, you must first be willing to live in accordance with His commandments. You must also study God's Word and be watchful for His signs. Finally, you should open yourself up to the Creator every day—beginning with this one—and you must have faith that He will soon reveal His plans to you.

Perhaps your vision of God's purpose for your life has been clouded by a wish list that you have expected God to dutifully fulfill. Perhaps you have fervently hoped that God would create a world that unfolds according to your wishes, not His. If so, you have probably experienced more disappointment than satisfaction and more frustration than peace. A better strategy is to conform your will to God's (and not to struggle vainly in an attempt to conform His will to yours).

Sometimes, God's plans and purposes may seem unmistakably clear to you. If so, push ahead. But other times, He may lead you through the wilderness before He directs you to the Promised Land. So be patient and keep seeking His will for your life. When you do, you'll be amazed at the marvelous things that an all-powerful, all-knowing God can do.

Some virtues cannot be produced in us
without affliction.

—

C. H. SPURGEON

MORE FROM GOD'S WORD ABOUT PURPOSE

Whatever you do, do all to the glory of God.

1 CORINTHIANS 10:31 NKJV

You're sons of Light, daughters of Day. We live under wide open skies and know where we stand. So let's not sleepwalk through life . . .

1 THESSALONIANS 5:5-6 MSG

We look at this Son and see the God who cannot be seen. We look at this Son and see God's original purpose in everything created.

COLOSSIANS 1:15 MSG

To everything there is a season, a time for every purpose under heaven.

ECCLESIASTES 3:1 NKJV

There is one thing I always do. Forgetting the past and straining toward what is ahead, I keep trying to reach the goal and get the prize for which God called me . . .

PHILIPPIANS 3:13-14 NCV

MORE POWERFUL IDEAS ABOUT PURPOSE

Underneath each trouble there is a faithful purpose.

C. H. SPURGEON

When the sovereign God brings us to nothing, it is to reroute our lives, not to end them.

CHARLES SWINDOLL

We should not be upset when unexpected and upsetting things happen. God, in His wisdom, means to make something of us which we have not yet attained, and He is dealing with us accordingly.

J. I. PACKER

A TIP FOR TODAY

God operates according to a perfect timetable. That timetable is His, not yours. So be patient.

Whatever clouds you face today, ask Jesus, the light of the world, to help you look behind the cloud to see His glory and His plans for you.

BILLY GRAHAM

A PRAYER FOR TODAY

Dear Lord, let Your purposes be my purposes. Let Your priorities be my priorities. Let Your will be my will. Let Your Word be my guide. And, let me grow in faith and in wisdom today and every day. Amen

TODAY'S THOUGHTS

My thoughts about the need to prayerfully ask God to direct my steps and guide my plans.

_____

_____

_____

_____

_____

_____

_____

_____

_____

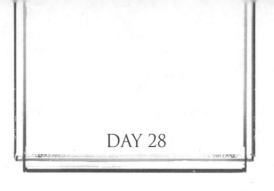

DAY 28

FINDING STRENGTH

*I can do all things through Christ
who strengthens me.*

—

PHILIPPIANS 4:13 NKJV

Faith not only can help you through a crisis,
it can help you to approach life after the hard times
with a whole new perspective. It can help you adopt
an outlook of hope and courage through
faith to face reality.

—

JOHN MAXWELL

God's love and support never changes. From the cradle to the grave, God has promised to give you the strength to meet any challenge. God has promised to lift you up and guide your steps if you let Him. God has promised that when you entrust your life to Him completely and without reservation, He will give you the courage to face any trial and the wisdom to live in His righteousness.

God's hand uplifts those who turn their hearts and prayers to Him. Will you count yourself among that number? Will you accept God's peace and wear God's armor against the temptations and distractions of our dangerous world? If you do, you can live courageously and optimistically, knowing that you have been forever touched by the loving, unfailing, uplifting hand of God.

HE IS SUFFICIENT

Of this you can be certain: God is sufficient to meet your needs. Period.

Do the demands of life seem overwhelming at times? If so, you must learn to rely not only upon your own resources, but also upon the promises of your Father in heaven. God will hold your hand and walk with you and your family if you let Him. So even if your circumstances are difficult, trust the Father.

God promises that He is "near to those who have a broken heart" (Psalm 34:18 NKJV). When we are troubled, we must turn to Him, and we must encourage our friends and family members to do likewise.

If you are discouraged by the inevitable demands of life here on earth, be mindful of this fact: the loving heart of God is sufficient to meet any challenge . . . including yours.

When trials come your way—as inevitably they will—
do not run away. Run to your God and Father.

—

KAY ARTHUR

MORE FROM GOD'S WORD ABOUT
FINDING STRENGTH

Be strong! We must prove ourselves strong for our people and for the cities of our God. May the Lord's will be done.

1 CHRONICLES 19:13 HCSB

And He said to me, "My grace is sufficient for you, for My strength is made perfect in weakness."

2 CORINTHIANS 12:9 NKJV

Finally, be strengthened by the Lord and by His vast strength.

EPHESIANS 6:10 HCSB

The LORD is my strength and my song . . .

EXODUS 15:2 NIV

Those who hope in the LORD will renew their strength. They will soar on wings like eagles; they will run and not grow weary, they will walk and not be faint.

ISAIAH 40:31 NIV

179

MORE POWERFUL IDEAS ABOUT FINDING STRENGTH

The same God who empowered Samson, Gideon, and Paul seeks to empower my life and your life, because God hasn't changed.

BILL HYBELS

A divine strength is given to those who yield themselves to the Father and obey what He tells them to do.

WARREN WIERSBE

If we take God's program, we can have God's power—not otherwise.

E. STANLEY JONES

A TIP FOR TODAY

If you're tempted to give up on yourself, remember that God will never give up on you. And with God in your corner, you have nothing to fear.

No matter how heavy the burden, daily strength is given, so I expect we need not give ourselves any concern as to what the outcome will be. We must simply go forward.

ANNIE ARMSTRONG

A PRAYER FOR TODAY

Lord, sometimes life is difficult. Sometimes, I am worried, weary, or heartbroken. But, when I lift my eyes to You, Father, You strengthen me. When I am weak, You lift me up. Today, I turn to You, Lord, for my strength, for my hope, and for my salvation. Amen

TODAY'S THOUGHTS

My thoughts about finding strength through God's promises.

_____

_____

_____

_____

_____

_____

_____

_____

_____

DAY 29

IN TOUGH TIMES, GOD TEACHES AND LEADS

Leave inexperience behind, and you will live;
pursue the way of understanding.

—

PROVERBS 9:6 HCSB

Your greatest ministry will likely come out
of your greatest hurt.

—

RICK WARREN

When it comes to your faith, God doesn't intend for you to stand still. He wants you to keep moving and growing. In fact, God's plan for you includes a lifetime of prayer, praise, and spiritual growth.

When we cease to grow, either emotionally or spiritually, we do ourselves and our loved ones a profound disservice. But, if we study God's Word, if we obey His commandments, and if we live in the center of His will, we will not be "stagnant" believers; we will, instead, be growing Christians . . . and that's exactly what God wants for our lives.

Many of life's most important lessons are painful to learn. During times of heartbreak and hardship, we must be courageous and we must be patient, knowing that in His own time, God will heal us if we invite Him into our hearts.

Spiritual growth need not take place only in times of adversity. We must seek to grow in our knowledge and love of the Lord every day that we live. In those quiet moments when we open our hearts to God, the One who made us keeps remaking us. He gives us direction, perspective, wisdom, and courage. The appropriate moment to accept those spiritual gifts is the present one.

Are you as mature as you're ever going to be? Hopefully not! When it comes to your faith, God doesn't intend for you to become "fully grown," at least not in this lifetime. In fact, God still has important lessons that He intends to teach you. So ask yourself this: What lesson is God trying to teach me today? And then go about the business of learning it.

WHERE IS GOD LEADING?

Whether we realize it or not, times of adversity can be times of intense personal and spiritual growth. Our difficult days are also times when we can learn and relearn some of life's most important lessons.

The next time you experience a difficult moment, a difficult day, or a difficult year, ask yourself this question: Where is God leading me? In times of struggle and sorrow, you can be certain that God is leading you to a place of His choosing. Your duty is to watch, to pray, to listen, and to follow.

MORE FROM GOD'S WORD ABOUT
SPIRITUAL GROWTH

For this reason we also, since the day we heard it, do not cease to pray for you, and to ask that you may be filled with the knowledge of His will in all wisdom and spiritual understanding

COLOSSIANS 1:9 NKJV

So let us stop going over the basics of Christianity again and again. Let us go on instead and become mature in our understanding.

HEBREWS 6:1 NLT

Run away from infantile indulgence. Run after mature righteousness—faith, love, peace—joining those who are in honest and serious prayer before God.

2 TIMOTHY 2:22 MSG

For You, O God, have tested us; You have refined us as silver is refined. You brought us into the net; You laid affliction on our backs. You have caused men to ride over our heads; we went through fire and through water; but You brought us out to rich fulfillment.

PSALM 66:10-12 NKJV

185

MORE POWERFUL IDEAS ABOUT
SPIRITUAL GROWTH

Let's thank God for allowing us to experience troubles that drive us closer to Him.

SHIRLEY DOBSON

It is a fact of Christian experience that life is a series of troughs and peaks. In his efforts to get permanent possession of a soul, God relies on the troughs more than the peaks. And, some of his special favorites have gone through longer and deeper troughs than anyone else.

PETER MARSHALL

Comfort and prosperity have never enriched the world as much as adversity has.

BILLY GRAHAM

A TIP FOR TODAY

Times of change can be times of growth.

Meditation is as silver; but tribulation is as fine gold.

C. H. SPURGEON

A PRAYER FOR TODAY

Dear Lord, when I open myself to You, I am blessed. Let me accept Your love and Your wisdom, Father. Show me Your way, and deliver me from the painful mistakes that I make when I stray from Your commandments. Let me live according to Your Word, and let me grow in my faith every day that I live. Amen

TODAY'S THOUGHTS

My thoughts about the rewards of growing emotionally and spiritually.

_____

_____

_____

_____

_____

_____

_____

_____

_____

DAY 30

FOLLOW HIM

*Then Jesus said to His disciples, "If anyone wants
to come with Me, he must deny himself,
take up his cross, and follow Me. For whoever
wants to save his life will lose it, but whoever
loses his life because of Me will find it."*

—

MATTHEW 16:24-25 HCSB

You who suffer take heart.
Christ is the answer to sorrow.

—

BILLY GRAHAM

Jesus walks with you. Are you walking with Him seven days a week, and not just on Sunday mornings? Are you a seven-day-a-week Christian who carries your faith with you to work each day, or do you try to keep Jesus at a "safe" distance when you're not sitting in church? Hopefully, you understand the wisdom of walking with Christ all day every day.

Jesus loved you so much that He endured unspeakable humiliation and suffering for you. How will you respond to Christ's sacrifice? Will you take up His cross and follow Him—during good times and tough times—or will you choose another path? When you place your hopes squarely at the foot of the cross, when you place Jesus squarely at the center of your life, you will be blessed.

Do you seek to fulfill God's purpose for your life? Do you seek spiritual abundance? Would you like to partake in "the peace that passes all understanding"? Then follow Christ. Follow Him by picking up His cross today and every day that you live. When you do, you will quickly discover that Christ's love has the power to change everything, including you.

YOUR ETERNAL JOURNEY

Eternal life is not an event that begins when you die. Eternal life begins when you invite Jesus into your heart right here on earth. So it's important to remember that God's plans for you are not limited to the ups and downs of everyday life. If you've allowed Jesus to reign over your heart, you've already begun your eternal journey.

Today, give praise to the Creator for His priceless gift, the gift of eternal life. And then, when you've offered Him your thanks and your praise, share His Good News with all who cross your path.

Sometimes we get tired of the burdens of life,
but we know that Jesus Christ will meet us
at the end of life's journey.
And, that makes all the difference.

—

BILLY GRAHAM

MORE FROM GOD'S WORD ABOUT FOLLOWING CHRIST

Then he told them what they could expect for themselves: "Anyone who intends to come with me has to let me lead."

LUKE 9:23 MSG

I've laid down a pattern for you. What I've done, you do.

JOHN 13:15 MSG

No one can serve two masters. Either he will hate the one and love the other, or he will be devoted to the one and despise the other.

MATTHEW 6:24 NIV

Whoever is not willing to carry the cross and follow me is not worthy of me. Those who try to hold on to their lives will give up true life. Those who give up their lives for me will hold on to true life.

MATTHEW 10:38-39 NCV

If anyone would come after me, he must deny himself and take up his cross and follow me.

MARK 8:34 NIV

MORE POWERFUL IDEAS ABOUT
FOLLOWING CHRIST

Jesus Christ is not a security from storms. He is perfect security in storms.

KATHY TROCCOLI

In the midst of the pressure and the heat, I am confident His hand is on my life, developing my faith until I display His glory, transforming me into a vessel of honor that pleases Him!

ANNE GRAHAM LOTZ

The Lord gets His best soldiers out of the highlands of affliction.

C. H. SPURGEON

A TIP FOR TODAY

If you want to be a little more like Jesus . . . learn about His teachings, follow in His footsteps, and obey His commandments.

God takes us through struggles and difficulties so that we might become increasingly committed to Him.

CHARLES SWINDOLL

192

A PRAYER FOR TODAY

Dear Jesus, because I am Your disciple, I will trust You, I will obey Your teachings, and I will share Your Good News. You have given me life abundant and life eternal, and I will follow You today and forever. Amen

TODAY'S THOUGHTS

My thoughts about the genuine joys and eternal rewards of following Jesus.

_____

_____

_____

_____

_____

_____

_____

_____

_____

We can all humbly say in
the sincerity of faith,
"I am loved; I am called;
I am secure."

—

FRANKLIN GRAHAM

APPENDIX

MORE FROM
GOD'S WORD

LEADERSHIP

For an overseer, as God's manager, must be blameless, not arrogant, not quick tempered, not addicted to wine, not a bully, not greedy for money.

TITUS 1:7 HCSB

According to the grace given to us, we have different gifts: If prophecy, use it according to the standard of faith; if service, in service; if teaching, in teaching; if exhorting, in exhortation; giving, with generosity; leading, with diligence; showing mercy, with cheerfulness.

ROMANS 12:6-8 HCSB

Shepherd God's flock among you, not overseeing out of compulsion but freely, according to God's will; not for the money but eagerly.

1 PETER 5:2 HCSB

And we exhort you, brothers: warn those who are lazy, comfort the discouraged, help the weak, be patient with everyone.

1 THESSALONIANS 5:14 HCSB

ABUNDANCE

I have come that they may have life, and that they may have it more abundantly.

JOHN 10:10 NKJV

And God is able to make every grace overflow to you, so that in every way, always having everything you need, you may excel in every good work.

2 CORINTHIANS 9:8 HCSB

Until now you have asked for nothing in My name. Ask and you will receive, that your joy may be complete.

JOHN 16:24 HCSB

*Come to terms with God and be at peace;
in this way good will come to you.*

JOB 22:21 HCSB

My cup runs over. Surely goodness and mercy shall follow me all the days of my life; and I will dwell in the house of the Lord forever.

PSALM 23:5-6 NKJV

DISCIPLESHIP

Anyone who listens to me is happy, watching at my doors every day, waiting by the posts of my doorway. For the one who finds me finds life and obtains favor from the Lord, but the one who sins against me harms himself; all who hate me love death.

PROVERBS 8:34-36 HCSB

He has told you men what is good and what it is the Lord requires of you: Only to act justly, to love faithfulness, and to walk humbly with your God.

MICAH 6:8 HCSB

Therefore, be imitators of God, as dearly loved children.

EPHESIANS 5:1 HCSB

We always pray for you that our God will consider you worthy of His calling, and will, by His power, fulfill every desire for goodness and the work of faith, so that the name of our Lord Jesus will be glorified by you, and you by Him, according to the grace of our God and the Lord Jesus Christ.

2 THESSALONIANS 1:11-12 HCSB

SILENCE

Happy is the man who finds wisdom, and the man who gains understanding.

PROVERBS 3:13 NKJV

I sought the Lord, and He heard me,
and delivered me from all my fears.

PSALM 34:4 NKJV

Be still, and know that I am God.

PSALM 46:10 NKJV

Be silent before the Lord and wait expectantly for Him.

PSALM 37:7 HCSB

In quietness and confidence shall be your strength.

ISAIAH 30:15 NKJV

I am not alone, because the Father is with Me.

JOHN 16:32 HCSB

MATURITY

*A wise man will hear, and will increase learning;
and a man of understanding shall attain
unto wise counsels.*

PROVERBS 1:5 KJV

Do not be conformed to this age, but be transformed by the renewing of your mind, so that you may discern what is the good, pleasing, and perfect will of God.

ROMANS 12:2 HCSB

When I was a child, I spoke like a child, I thought like a child, I reasoned like a child. When I became a man, I put aside childish things.

1 CORINTHIANS 13:11 HCSB

Consider it a great joy, my brothers, whenever you experience various trials, knowing that the testing of your faith produces endurance. But endurance must do its complete work, so that you may be mature and complete, lacking nothing.

JAMES 1:2-4 HCSB

EXAMPLE

Love and truth form a good leader; sound leadership is founded on loving integrity.

PROVERBS 20:28 MSG

You should be an example to the believers in speech, in conduct, in love, in faith, in purity.

1 TIMOTHY 4:12 HCSB

Therefore since we also have such a large cloud of witnesses surrounding us, let us lay aside every weight and the sin that so easily ensnares us, and run with endurance the race that lies before us.

HEBREWS 12:1 HCSB

Set an example of good works yourself, with integrity and dignity in your teaching.

TITUS 2:7 HCSB

Do everything without grumbling and arguing, so that you may be blameless and pure.

PHILIPPIANS 2:14-15 HCSB

ANGER

Everyone must be quick to hear, slow to speak, and slow to anger, for man's anger does not accomplish God's righteousness.

JAMES 1:19-20 HCSB

A patient person [shows] great understanding, but a quick-tempered one promotes foolishness.

PROVERBS 14:29 HCSB

But now you must also put away all the following: anger, wrath, malice, slander, and filthy language from your mouth.

COLOSSIANS 3:8 HCSB

Don't let your spirit rush to be angry, for anger abides in the heart of fools.

ECCLESIASTES 7:9 HCSB

All bitterness, anger and wrath, insult and slander must be removed from you, along with all wickedness. And be kind and compassionate to one another, forgiving one another, just as God also forgave you in Christ.

EPHESIANS 4:31-32 HCSB

GENEROSITY

The generous soul will be made rich, and he who waters will also be watered himself.

PROVERBS 11:25 NKJV

Freely you have received, freely give.

MATTHEW 10:8 NKJV

As each one has received a gift, minister it to one another, as good stewards of the manifold grace of God.

1 PETER 4:10 NKJV

But this I say: He who sows sparingly will also reap sparingly, and he who sows bountifully will also reap bountifully. So let each one give as he purposes in his heart, not grudgingly or of necessity; for God loves a cheerful giver.

2 CORINTHIANS 9:6-7 NKJV

Cast your bread upon the waters, for you will find it after many days.

ECCLESIASTES 11:1 NKJV

DREAMS

Now may the God of hope fill you with all joy and peace in believing, so that you may overflow with hope by the power of the Holy Spirit.

ROMANS 15:13 HCSB

Where there is no vision, the people perish.

PROVERBS 29:18 KJV

Be of good courage, and he shall strengthen your heart, all ye that hope in the LORD.

PSALM 31:24 KJV

Therefore, as we have opportunity, we must work for the good of all, especially for those who belong to the household of faith.

GALATIANS 6:10 HCSB

But as it is written: What no eye has seen and no ear has heard, and what has never come into a man's heart, is what God has prepared for those who love Him.

1 CORINTHIANS 2:9 HCSB

GOD'S TIMING

Wait for the Lord; be courageous and
let your heart be strong. Wait for the Lord.

PSALM 27:14 HCSB

He said to them, "It is not for you to know times or periods that
the Father has set by His own authority."

ACTS 1:7 HCSB

He has made everything appropriate in its time. He has also put
eternity in their hearts, but man cannot discover the work God
has done from beginning to end.

ECCLESIASTES 3:11 HCSB

Therefore the Lord is waiting to show you mercy, and is rising
up to show you compassion, for the Lord is a just God. Happy
are all who wait patiently for Him.

ISAIAH 30:18 HCSB

For My thoughts are not your thoughts, and your ways are not
My ways. For as heaven is higher than earth, so My ways are
higher than your ways, and My thoughts than your thoughts.

ISAIAH 55:8-9 HCSB

ENCOURAGING OTHERS

*I want their hearts to be encouraged and joined together in love,
so that they may have all the riches of assured understanding,
and have the knowledge of God's mystery—Christ.*

COLOSSIANS 2:2 HCSB

*And let us be concerned about one another
in order to promote love and good works.*

HEBREWS 10:24 HCSB

*Carry one another's burdens; in this way you will fulfill the law
of Christ.*

GALATIANS 6:2 HCSB

*But encourage each other daily, while it is still called today, so
that none of you is hardened by sin's deception.*

HEBREWS 3:13 HCSB

*Anxiety in a man's heart weighs it down, but a good word
cheers it up.*

PROVERBS 12:25 HCSB

LOVE

As in water face reflects face, so a man's heart reveals the man.

PROVERBS 27:19 NKJV

No one has greater love than this, that someone would lay down his life for his friends.

JOHN 15:13 HCSB

Though I speak with the tongues of men and of angels, but have not love, I have become sounding brass or a clanging cymbal.

1 CORINTHIANS 13:1 NKJV

Dear friends, if God loved us in this way, we also must love one another.

1 JOHN 4:11 HCSB

Above all, keep your love for one another at full strength, since love covers a multitude of sins.

1 PETER 4:8 HCSB

And if you believe,
you will receive whatever you ask for
in prayer.

MATTHEW 21:22 HCSB